KEVIN McCLOUD'S
GRAND TOUR OF EUROPE

KEVIN McCLOUD'S
GRAND TOUR OF EUROPE

Kevin McCloud

Text Consultant **Isabel Allen**

Principal Photography by **Hugo MacGregor**

WEIDENFELD & NICOLSON

Contents

Introduction

I am no expert on the Grand Tour. For authority you could look to any number of books on the subject, most of which are extensively packed with contemporary accounts from monied aristocrats of how the wheels of their carriages fell off and the precise details of their mercury poultices applied to relieve the effects of syphilis. But these books are usually restricted in their subject to one century, country or city. When we set out to make the television series for Channel 4, it was clear to me that a comprehensive set of programmes covering three centuries and every facet of the Tour would be fruitless and unwatchable. So would a dry history of the art and architecture of the period. For a brilliant read on the buildings and culture of Europe, look no further than Kenneth Clark's entertaining accompaniment to his 1960s series *Civilisation*. Or find any one of John Summerson's books. They will show and tell you far more than any series can.

We took a more cursive and personal route. The series comprises four one-hour films and I was fascinated by four big stories, four big ideas in the history of Big Ideas that I've always found compelling and which have made it into this book. The first is that of my biggest architectural hero, Inigo Jones, and how, as a young artist, later turned architect, he travelled through Northern Italy in the early seventeenth century to study, record and import the ideas and style of the great Andrea Palladio – ideas that were to remain barren in England until Colen

Campbell and Lord Burlington revived them a century later and sparked the Palladian style of building that we simply know now as 'Georgian'.

The second treads in the imaginary footsteps of Sir Christopher Wren, who, in designing St Paul's Cathedral, never stepped foot on the continent beyond Paris. This is a detective story, linking the inspirational buildings that Wren, in the 1660s and 1670s, knew from accounts, friends and engravings: the major domes of Italy that would lead to the creation of one of Britain's most revered symbolic structures. A domological detective story in fact. With occasional stories of drunkenness and syphilis thrown in for roughage.

The third episode springs lightly in the footsteps of a canny Scottish design dynasty, the Adam family. Set against the discovery of Pompeii and Herculaneum, the growth of Grand Tourism, trade in artefacts and statues, revelations of a priapic cult and archaeological skullduggery, this is the tale of how Robert and James Adam imported newly discovered ideas and designs from the classical world and then set about making money from them by reproducing everything from Roman door handles to entire neoclassical houses. Well, almost. This is the tale of how, in the 1760s, Design, for the first time, sort of became Brand.

And in our final episode – and section of this book – I set off to Greece to discover what lay behind all this new archaeology. The inspiration that was the classical world of Homer and Plato, a world which sparked a Greek revival in Britain for which the fashionable set just went wild in the early decades of the nineteenth century. I went, only to realize, as Grand Tourists had done (people like Cockerell, Stuart and Revett and Lord Elgin), that behind the primitive temples placed on top of mountains and in front of caves lay something more primal and even more inspirational, the mountains and caves themselves.

The entire journey has been both a revisit of my own youth (I spent a year or so exploring Italy and studying there) and a blessed opportunity for me to live out the adventures of my own architectural heroes – people who changed the face of Britain by importing radical foreign ideas that often met with opposition and suspicion. Ideas like the Georgian terraced house; squares; the notion you could create organized public spaces or build fountains and statuary for pleasure; ideas which have completely altered how our towns and cities look. That seemed to me to be a decent reason for going – making the connection between the original inspiration and how where we live now looks. On my last trip, from Greece across the Alps into the extraordinary mountainous beauty of Switzerland to see glaciers eroded by climate change, my awareness has been sharpened of how our twenty-first-century rejection of industrialization in favour of the Ecological movement mirrors the early-nineteenth-century rejection of the Enlightenment in favour of the emerging Romantic movement. Both of these new ideas are connected through their emphasis on the natural environment and awe for the power of nature – expressed in the idea of the sublime as much as that of sustainability.

And because this is a personal journey, because this is a journey from place to place, because we flit occasionally from the seventeenth to the nineteenth century if the story of a place on my travels demands it, there are obvious holes. I make no apology for not including any proper reference to baroque art or architecture. We see its most powerful expression incipient in the realization of St Paul's and we move on. This is not a comprehensive history of architecture, after all. No apology either for nothing more than a mention of Lord Burlington, who arrived back in England with dozens of cases of artefacts and statuary and who almost single-handedly launched 'Palladianism' or at least a Palladio-inspired movement of design in early eighteenth-century Britain that was one of the most powerful shapers of our high streets. No. Maybe I'd have given him time if we'd been asked to make five programmes. I might even revisit his story one day. And no apology either for the omission of French seventeenth-century monumental architecture, the rococo, Gothic Revival, or coverage of the Totteridge curly-wurly lamppost movement. They're all for a drier, different kind of arts programme. And, as I've said, there are plenty of good books out there on these subjects already.

Acknowledgements

Every ounce of thanks, however, must go to the team that produced the series and this book: Debbie Woska and Michael Dover at Orion for finessing and crafting this volume; Jane Turnbull and Tracey MacLeod, my agents, for standing for all that is righteous and expensable; Binkie Jackson for model-making; Gina Pelham for research not least into the Pelham family archive; Hugo MacGregor for photography, research, anecdotes, directing and editing the series; Michael Waldman, our producer, director and fixer of first-class upgrades extraordinaire, for telling me what to do, for more anecdotes, all entertaining, mostly nothing to do with the series and for standing up for culture, good storytelling and strong ideas; our crew, comprising Andy Muggleton, Chris Syner and Colin Fox, for relentlessly holding heavy pieces of equipment up in the air and capturing beauty with them; all at Silver River, especially Daisy Goodwin, our loving curator and Dan Adamson our caring executive producer; Caterina for tireless organization on location and Elena for tireless research. A particular thank you to Channel 4 for broadcasting the series under the watchful eye of Liam Humphries and to Sue Murphy for commissioning it with such passion and zeal.

And finally, heartfelt relief and thanks to Isabel Allen, colleague and friend, for helping to pen this book. It's customary not to acknowledge aid in the writing department but without her words it would be a considerably shorter read.

Page 6 Venice, early morning. The fretwork façades of the *palazzi* were a device to save weight, as well as a visual delight.

Previous pages Wren's double-decker of Corinthian columns and twin Tempiettos on the west front of St Paul's Cathedral.

Right The monumental remains of the Parthenon, the model for so many equally monumental civic buildings around the world.

Below The Fiat 500 – a dead ringer for the car I used to drive years ago when living in Italy.

From London to **Paris** – a crash course in Continental Culture

Paris, the first stop on any tour, attracted Grand Tourists
in droves; in 1787 3,760 Englishmen visited the city in
just six weeks. They didn't come for the architecture.

A congested jumble of narrow, crooked streets and pointed gables and spires, its Gothic townscape had been dismissed by the great Italian architect Bernini in the 1660s as a collection of chimneys resembling nothing so much as the spiked instrument used for carding wool. Bernini was famously rude about almost everything, but British visitors were minded to agree. Armed with an education in Latin and the classics, they came to the Continent in search of classical enlightenment and to an extent they regarded Paris as an architectural backwater, a city which by the end of the seventeenth century had become populated with formal buildings that seemed like large defensive blocks with a smidgen of classical surface decoration. Italy, with its classical architecture and antique ruins, was the undisputed focus of the Tour. The French interpretation of the classical world seemed strangely wooden. What the Grand Tourist wanted was the romance of classical literature, the heroism and passion of the *Aeneid* and of Horace brought to life in the streets and ruins of the Italian peninsula.

And these interrelationships remain the same today in my view. Paris is now an immensely cultured city, formal, well laid-out and impressive. Its architecture, ancient and modern, still reeks of the concentration of power and composure: the very effect that centuries of French bureaucrats have wanted to create. But passion? Romance? Where are they? There may be beauty in Paris, but for unbridled, loose sensuality you have to look further south.

Historically, visitors didn't even come to France for the food: it was oily, garlicky, over-spiced and over-sauced and frogs' legs were viewed as a poor substitute for good, honest Protestant roast beef. They came instead for a crash course in Continental culture at the first stop on foreign soil and an opportunity to acquire the requisite manners and appearance for entry into foreign courts. Britain had always mistrusted Continental sophisticates, but on the Tour one joined them. In Paris, Tobias Smollett in *Travels Through France and Italy* wrote 'the Tourist cannot appear until he has undergone a total metamorphosis.' You 'Frenchified' yourself with silks from Lyon, brocade from Les Gobelins, perfume, powdered wigs, a new coat – and became the *Milord* on the Continent. And you stocked up with perfume – a travelling essential when there's no knowing when you're going to get your next bath. Paris was the centre of the perfume industry; *fleurs d'oranger* and *eau de lavande,* which offered protection against bedbugs, were the smells of the age. Such 'Frenchification' of course provoked a lot of suspicion on British soil about the emasculating influence of Continental ways. Smollett observed that visitors aped not only the fashionable dress and manners of the Parisians,

Tucking into a big bowl of oily, garlicky frogs' legs.

Left Paris offered the Grand Tourist a crash course in dressing like a Continental sophisticate. In his *Travels Through France and Italy*, published in 1766, the Scottish author Tobias Smollett accused the English not only of aping dress and manners but also of ostentation, indecency and unmanly subjection to the whims of women.

Above My own take on this time-honoured ritual is to visit Paris' most experimental men's fashion shop: L'Eclaireur's Cabinet des Curiosités, where I am styled in modern fashionable clothes…

but also their ostentation, indecency and, worse still, their unmanly subjection to the whims of Frenchwomen. Many a young gent returned to Britain more foppish than expected.

Place des Vosges

But in Paris they could preen to their heart's content. Grand Tourists joined fashionable Parisians at the Place des Vosges, originally called Place Royale, *the* place to be seen and historically the site of an endless whirl of tournaments and duels. The rules of modern fencing were being established in the eighteenth century, not least in order to establish an etiquette of duelling to avoid both combatants getting killed, and lessons with a fencing master were deemed part of the process of becoming a gentleman. As well as being an important social accomplishment, it was crucial that travellers were prepared for attacks by brigands on the epic journey ahead.

Built by Henri IV from 1605 to 1612 to designs probably by Baptiste du Cerceau, the Place des Vosges represented a concerted effort to create coherent cosmopolitan splendour in a city that was generally claustrophobic, chaotic and cramped. This was the first formal square as we know it with terraces of identical

Eighteenth-century engraving of a fencing lesson. The rules of engagement were still being established, and combatants did not wear masks.

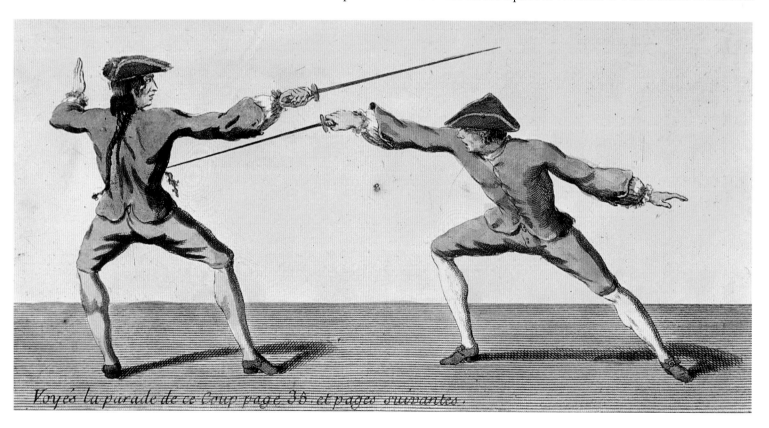

Voyés la parade de ce Coup page 38 et pages suivantes.

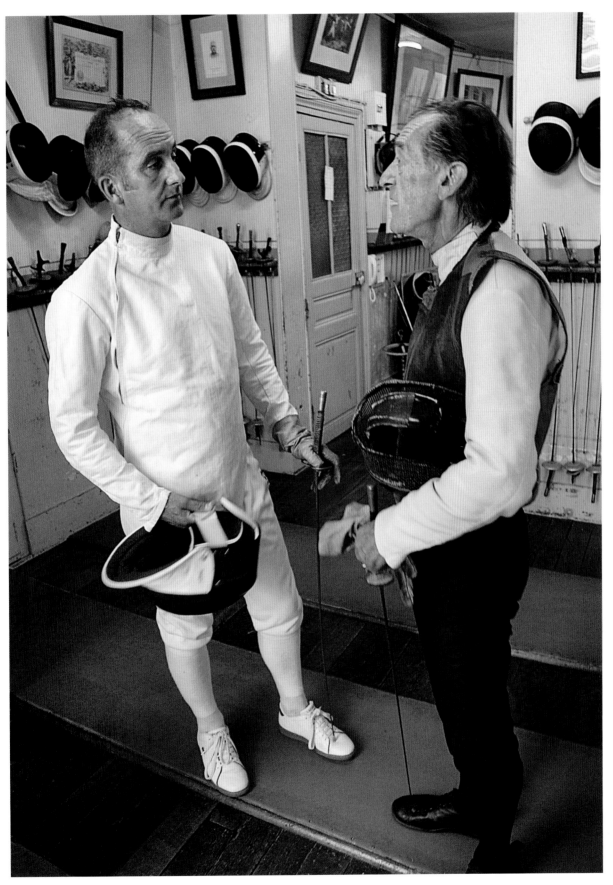

Lessons with a fencing master were part of the process of becoming a gentleman. As well as being an important social accomplishment, it was important that travellers were prepared for attacks by brigands on the journey ahead.

houses on four sides. It was built for the Parisian nobility, who had always resided in country châteaux or 'hotels' (private houses) scattered throughout the city, but here their dwellings were expressed as constituent parts of an over-arching composition. In a radical departure from the norm the thirty-eight houses were all built to the same design – red brick and cream stone façades, steep slate roofs and dormer windows and a ground floor vaulted arcade – creating a unified backdrop for the pageantry of the great court. And a shopping arcade. The superiority of the monarchy is clearly expressed by King's and Queen's pavilions, which punctuate the roofline, and sit above the triple-arched gateways at the north and south ends of the square. Politically the Place put the nobility in their place; architecturally it put Paris on the map.

Regal posturing apart, the square – and at 140m x 140m it *is* a true square – represents the city's first real attempt at town planning and was the prototype for countless city squares across Europe. Since opening with great aplomb, with a celebration of the wedding of Louis XIII and Anne of Austria, it was an essential part of the Grand Tour itinerary. I have always been fascinated by the square's uncanny resemblance to Covent Garden Piazza when it was first built in the

The city's first attempt at town planning and the prototype for countless city squares all over Europe the Place des Vosges was once the meeting place of all Paris. It has lost its original sparkle and is now distinctly down at heel, but still asserts the coherence and grandeur it had then.

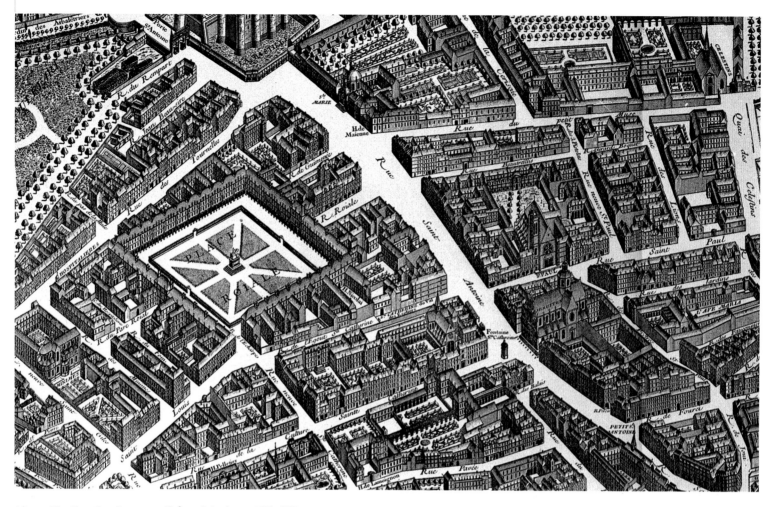

Above The Place Royale, now Place des Vosges, as shown in Turgot's plan of Paris drawn in 1731.

Below Inigo Jones, 1573–1653, Englishman, Grand Tourist, architect and the man who introduced classical architecture to Britain.

1630s. And there's clearly an influence here because one of my building heroes, the English theatre designer and first proper architect in this country, Inigo Jones, was, it seems, the hidden master-planning hand behind Covent Garden. Jones had toured France and Italy in 1596 but undertook a second Grand Tour of Italy between April 1613 and Autumn 1614, visiting Paris on the way home.

The son of a cloth worker, Jones worked for King Christian IV of Denmark and for Queen Anne (King Christian's sister and the wife of England's James I) as a designer of costumes and scenery for court masques before becoming Surveyor of Works to Henry, Prince of Wales in 1610. The appointment came to an abrupt end with the prince's death in 1612 but the death of the king's Surveyor of Works, Simon Basil, in 1613 brought the promise of an even more distinguished role. For Jones, his second Grand Tour, taken in the company of Thomas Howard, Earl of Arundel, and his wife Aletheia, offered a chance to complete his self-education as a classical architect before returning to England to become Surveyor of Works first to James I and subsequently to Charles I.

The role, which was essentially that of chief architect to the Crown, lasted from

1615 until the outbreak of civil war in 1642. Jones exercised significant influence over London's development, but he built little of his own design and generally found his progressive, classical ideas disliked at court, where the concocted mannerist styles of the sixteenth century kept hanging around. Covent Garden was perhaps an exception. Once the site of a convent, the land had been gifted to the Bedford family by Henry VIII after the Reformation as a token of gratitude for service to the royal house. Around 1630 the fourth Earl of Bedford decided that the time had come to exploit the convent garden, or Covent Garden, for speculative development – on a stately scale. In a plan that was to be mimicked by other London landowners, Bedford laid out the square to the north of his own back garden, leaving the southern edge of the development open so as to allow in light and a view from his own house.

Place Royale on British soil. Covent Garden Piazza, the first London square of the seventeenth century, was the first housing project in the city to be organized through the use of the classical orders. The ground floor arcade was conceived as public space, reminiscent of the classical forum.

The first of the newly built London squares of the seventeenth century, Covent Garden is credited as London's first stab at formal town planning and was the first housing project in the city to be organized through the use of the classical orders: Jones' own Doric church there is the first public Protestant church in England and the first classically designed church too. The terraced houses were in the Ionic order and the very idea of a public square can be clearly traced back to its Continental roots. Designed as a classical forum, with arcades and a public meeting place in the portico of the church, the piazza was more classical – even more *Italian* – than the Place des Vosges – suggesting influence from wider travels: Vicenza's palace façades; Livorno's piazza and church. Both of which Jones would have seen.

The Covent Garden development included seventeen arcaded houses, thought to have been designed by the supervising architect Isaac de Caus, on the north and east sides. Jones' Church of St Paul lay to the west. Though lower than the other buildings, the church was the most prominent element in the square thanks to its monumental portico and temple front. A low wall bordered the gardens of the Bedford estate to the south. The housing was an exercise in unabashed façadism; a successful attempt to apply regal bombast to commercial ends. As at the Place des Vosges, identical units combined to form a composition of palace-like proportions; the same colour of brick and stone were used; the window proportions were copied and similar dormer windows inserted; there was even a matching ground floor arcade. Behind the façades, tenants were free to arrange their quarters exactly as they pleased.

While the Place des Vosges drew on classical precedent to convey the gravitas of the court, Covent Garden used it to create a shrine to commerce. The Place des Vosges became the scene of knightly sports and tournaments; Covent Garden became a vegetable market, a valuable addition to the Bedford family fortune. For all its monumentality it remained, at heart, a place to trade.

But its influence was profound. Jones didn't just introduce proper classicism to Britain. He introduced town planning. He didn't just copy the works of the puritanical classicist Andrea Palladio, he developed and adapted the style to our culture, albeit 100 years before we were ready for it. And he left another, quieter legacy: the terraced house. The streets we all live in have grown from that idea expressed in Covent Garden. A century later Robert Adam was drawing on the same language to the north in Bloomsbury and to the south in the Adelphi, though his houses were even grander – without the shops and with a pediment in the middle of the façade so that they truly looked like large palaces. Our homes and our streets wouldn't be what they are if it weren't for Jones – and the Grand Tour he undertook.

Above Covent Garden Piazza today. Though none of the houses survive, St Paul's Church still stands. Its monumental portico remains a popular meeting place.

Opposite Covent Garden c.1726 by Pieter Angillis. For all its classical pretensions Covent Garden became famous as a flourishing vegetable market. Designed as a speculative commercial development, it remained, at heart, a place to trade.

By Felucca to **Genoa** – the first sight and taste of Italy

Finding the 'right' accomodation in the palazzi
of the New Town, and exploring the seamier side
of the medieval Old Town.

My first Italian stop was Genoa – Genova in Italian – by boat of course. Italy in the seventeenth century was divided into different principalities and two republics: Genoa and Venice. As powerful maritime and trading centres both were seen as models for a new England which was determined to become, and on its way to becoming, its own maritime power. Between 1550 and 1650 Genoa, or 'La Superba' as it was called by Petrarch, was the banking centre of Europe. The established dynasties of ship owners and merchants had become bankers to the King of Spain, commanding high rates of interest which were paid with silver and gold from Mexico and Peru. After the defeat, and subsequent bankruptcy, of Spain in 1630 Genoa became a city in decline, but the art and architecture commissioned during its Golden Age left a legacy which made it an essential port of call on the Grand Tour.

Getting there

To avoid the mountains, which were viewed as hazardous and malevolent, Grand Tourists would travel south to Marseilles or Cannes, where a felucca boat would be hired to take them to Genoa (my felucca was a small single-masted wooden sailing boat). But even sea travel was not without its hazards. Seasickness was a common complaint, alleviated – with varying degrees of success – by chewing on ginger or

The dark medieval streets of Genoa's port are so narrow that it has to be explored on foot. Grand Tourists would at least have had the option of a sedan chair.

John Mitford wrote of the felucca in 1776 'These Mediterranean vessels are not formed for bad weather and they are manned by not very skilful mariners' but conceded that 'The beauty of the rocky coast, and the variety of its scenery afford some recompense for the tedious passage.'

peppermint. Once on dry land sufferers could follow Dr Johnson's advice that the best cure to seasickness is to 'find a good oak tree and wrap your arms around it.' Aside from seasickness and stormy weather travellers had to contend with piracy, not to mention the Italian sailors – who were generally conceived to be lacking in both competence and courage. John Molesworth, English envoy in Turin from 1720–25, remarked that 'No mariners in the world are so cowardly as the Italians in general, but especially the Genoese; so that upon the least appearance of a rough sea, they run into the first creek when their feluccas are sometimes wind-bound for a month.'

Staying there

The first challenge on arrival was to secure the right lodgings; right in terms of appropriateness to one's standing. There were some ninety *palazzi* prepared to accommodate foreign guests – but turning up on the doorstep was out of the question. The owners, fed up with fighting amongst themselves, had passed responsibility for allocating rooms to the municipality, who implemented a booking system governed by a strict pecking order. Prior to arrival, Grand Tourists were classified according to title, status and dress, and sent to equivalent lodgings drawn from a list of *palazzi* that could house foreign tourists. List A classified the highest ranking; List B for the next step down; and so on.

Left and Below Strada Nuova, a collection of mannerist and baroque aristocratic houses and palaces, is considered to be the first example of a coherent Renaissance urban development project. Much admired by Grand Tourists, the 'New Street' was *the* place to stay.

The place to stay was Strada Nuova – 'New Street', a collection of mannerist and baroque aristocratic houses and palaces (Palazzi dei Rolli) belonging to the city's leading families and considered the first example of a coherent Renaissance urban development project. First opened in 1550 and completed in 1716, it was much admired by Grand Tourists. Richard Lassell, in his *Description of Italy*, voiced the opinion that 'The strada nova for a spirit surpasseth in beauty and buildings all the streets in Europe that ever I saw any where; and if it did but hold out some rate a little longer it might be called the Queen Street of the world. Ordinary houses are out of countenance and dare not appear in this street, where every house is a palace and every palace as beautiful as marble pillars and paintings can make it.' Rubens, who made numerous trips to Genoa in the early 1600s, collated a collection of plans, sections and elevation of its *palazzi* with the stated intention of providing Belgium (or the Spanish Netherlands) with 'models of houses suitable for gentlemen rather than princes'. When, in the early seventeenth century, the City Senate conducted a detailed census of private houses that could play host to illustrious visitors, the palaces of Strada Nuova were deemed to be the only quarters worthy of an emperor or pope.

But if visitors were dazzled by the splendours of the New Town, they were rather less impressed by the medieval Old Town. To Grand Tourists, the gothic architecture of the Cattedrale di San Lorenzo, striped with a black and white marble licorice-allsorts façade and interior, was – and is – an important landmark. But its jumble

A jumble of historic styles, the Cattedrale di San Lorenzo in Genoa's Old Town found little favour with Grand Tourists, who viewed it as a legacy of a more barbaric age.

of historical styles, where baroque piles on top of Romanesque and Renaissance sits cheek-by-jowl with Gothic, seemed superstitious and ignorant. The very word 'Gothic', when applied to architecture, was a pejorative term used as early as the 1530s by Giorgio Vasari to describe culture that was considered rude and barbaric. In any case, Grand Tourists had plenty of Gothic architecture back in England.

The dark corners, cramped conditions and narrow twisting streets of old Genoa were dirty and disease-ridden. Their poverty, as was the case in any city, powerfully signified breakdown and social disorder. And not without reason. The double whammy of London's Great Plague, which had claimed 100,000 lives between 1665 and 1666, and Great Fire, which destroyed 13,200 houses in 1666, brought the perils of medieval cities sharply into focus, prompting Charles II to issue a series of mandates on issues such as sanitation, construction standards and the widening of streets. Afterwards, educated Tourists came in search of the new, ordered, carriage-friendly, airy town planning associated with a Golden Age of learning and refinement. In the early 1600s, Inigo Jones had come before these ideas had taken root.

Danger and women

As to moral disorder the medieval streets did allow for the concealment of all sorts of sins. Genoa was seen as a dangerous town, where murders went unchecked and sex was available on every corner. Not that the latter was necessarily seen as such a bad thing by British visitors. The Grand Tour was as much about gaining sexual experience and 'becoming a man' as it was about looking for ancient Rome – an opportunity for young aristos to throw themselves into the mess, dirt and stink of real life away from home soil.

Though nothing if not game – even married women cavorted openly with male companions – Genoese women, by all accounts, were something of a disappointment. Hester Thrale (1741–1821), a close friend of Samuel Johnson's, warned that 'The generality of the women here are the most ugly hags in the universe. Their heads are of a monstrous size, their complexion swarthy and olive-coloured, their features large and their mouths exceeding wide…what sort of beauty is suited to the Italian taste I know not, but I'm certain an Englishman would be shocked at the sight of them.' He sounds biased, but not as much as the Reverend John Swinton (1703–1777), English chaplain at Livorno, who dismissed Genoese women as 'the proudest creatures in the universe, and most intolerably and insufferably insolent, especially to their husbands'. Perhaps it's not surprising that many Grand Tourists spent just one day in Genoa before going on their way.

A visit to the opera in **Parma** – and making Parmesan cheese, a staple of the Grand Tourists

Parma was an introduction to music, and opera in particular, an Italian invention, and stocking up on chunks of Parmesan cheese for the journey ahead.

From 1545, when the Farnese pope Paul III presented Parma and Piacenza to his illegitimate son, Parma was a small principality governed by the Farnese family from the Farnese Palace. When the last male of the Farnese line died in 1731 the combined Duchy of Parma and Piacenza was given to the House of Bourbon. Like many of these small court states, Parma was a city of spectacle and a hotbed of the arts. Grand Tourists popped into the Romanesque cathedral to marvel at the twelfth-century sculpture by Benedetto Antelami and Antonio da Correggio's *Assumption of the Virgin*, a sixteenth-century fresco masterpiece. But the real attraction was the court, where they went to enjoy Farnese theatre and court entertainment.

Grand Tourists who visited Parma before 1732 might have been extremely lucky and caught a performance in the beautiful baroque Teatro Farnese, which occupied the first floor of the Palazzo della Pilotta. Built in 1618 by the architect Giovanni Battista Aleotti (1546–1636), it is regarded as the prototype of the modern playhouse and is the first surviving theatre with a permanent proscenium arch. A large U-shaped parterre was designed to accommodate a range of courtly entertainments including dancing and royal processions. It could even be flooded for water spectacles, though in the event it wasn't used that much at all. The theatre opened in 1628 with a six-hour performance of *Mercury and Mars* with

Previous pages Built in 1618, the baroque Teatro Farnese in the Palazzo della Pilotta is regarded as the prototype of the modern playhouse.

From 1637, when the first public opera house opened in Venice, opera ceased to be the exclusive privilege of royalty and the court. Opera houses such as the Teatro Reale in Turin (below) and Teatro La Fenice in Venice (bottom) became a popular attraction on the Grand Tour.

Teatro della Fenice a Venezia

music by Monteverdi, but was used only nine times before being left to decay a century later. It was eventually reopened in 1913 but had to be rebuilt following its destruction during the Second World War.

Music was one of the major passions of Grand Tourists and almost as big a draw in Italy as painting and architecture. Opera started in Italy in the sixteenth century – Claudio Monteverdi's *L'Orfeo*, produced in Mantua in 1607, was one of the earliest operas – and originated as a new music form for court spectacle. From 1637, when the first public opera house opened in Venice, it ceased to be the exclusive privilege of royalty and the court; everybody was welcome as long as they could afford to pay. Some tourists sought to attend the opera in all the towns they visited, with many visitors altering their route to attend specific performances or, more accurately, to hear specific singers. Opera singers were the subject of fevered adulation and composers were commissioned to create operas to show the particular capabilities of the performers to the best possible advantage; the celebrated castrato Farinelli was a particular draw. An anonymous visitor to Turin in 1782 commented 'the music is never attended to by the people of the country unless a new opera and the first representation perhaps – or a favourite air by a favourite singer – it appears to be rather a general *conversazione*, and that on a high key.' Numerous Grand Tourists complained about the Italian audiences being too noisy. The famous actor David Garrick, who visited Italy with his wife in 1763–64, was astounded by the audience noise at the Turin opera in 1763 and particularly surprised that players engaged in conversation with members of the audience.

I went to the opera in Parma when I was there to see a riveting performance of *Lucia di Lammermoor*, an opera written for a public audience and one which held its particular audience that night spellbound. But for a Grand Tourist an evening at the opera was a raucous affair. Performances lasted many hours, during which the audience dined, drank, gossiped, played games and generally made so much noise that composers eventually adopted the convention of introducing loud chords (*coups d'archet*) to let the audience know when an important aria was about to begin. Composers were also obliged to ensure that the music would drown out the noise generated by the elaborate machinery used to create particular special effects.

By the eighteenth century the British back home worried about the influence of Italian music on their new generation. Opera was held to be an unnatural art – the press strongly criticized the popularity of Italian castrati and launched attacks on the supposed abandonment of British culture in favour of a pernicious, effeminate import. Adam Walker, touring Italy in 1787, launched a savage attack on opera:

'Of all the seminaries appropriated to the wise purpose of propagating folly, none ever equalled the Italian Opera: Here, indeed the god Fashion displays his mental triumph! Reason is led into captivity by the ears! Virtue and public spirit take opiates from the hands of Circe! – and effeminacy, lewdness, and perverted ideas gambol in the train! Calling it a school of softness and debility…that makes men – like Venetians.' Grand Tourists were warned not to mingle with opera singers – advice which many ignored.

I didn't arrive by accident in Parma. My route through northern Italy from one City Republic to another allowed me this small diversion; not just to see the opera or gawp at the awesome Farnese Palazzo, but to make cheese. Organic farm-produced Parmesan cheese, which is one of the world's finest and worth a 100-mile detour for. Parmezan, as it was known – or Parmigiano Reggiano – is the pride of Parma and the surrounding area. During its 800-year history it has amassed an impressive collection of accolades. In the medieval allegorical work *The Decameron*, thought to have been written between 1350 and 1353, the Italian author Giovanni Boccaccio dreams of 'a mountain of grated Parmesan cheese on

Parmesan production in the Po Valley. Its success is attributed to happy healthy cows, fed exclusively on grass and hay, and to the patience of the populace. Cheeses are dried, turned and aged over a period of one to four years. It is like watching alchemal gold being formed.

The regulating body, the Consorzio del Parmagiano Reggiano, ensures that traditional methods of Parmesan production are maintained. The evening milking is left overnight before the cream is skimmed off to make mascarpone. The milk is then mixed with the morning's milking in huge copper cauldrons before rennet is added.

PARMA in **Valli e Sapori**
percorso enogastronomico
...valliesapori.it

top of which there were people who did nothing but make macaroni and ravioli'. The playwright Molière begged for a chunk of it on his deathbed. Napoleon was a big fan and Samuel Pepys famously buried his Parmesan in the garden to protect it from the Great Fire of London. Since the cheese was taxed on entry to each of the eight states it had to cross before reaching English soil it was a costly indulgence for English gourmands.

Its appeal lies in its unique flavour – deemed to embody 'umami', the so-called fifth or 'savoury' taste, although as I discovered on tasting, after 24 months the cheese develops sweet granular crystals. It is also pretty unique among cheeses as one that consumes all the lactose from the curds and so it's acceptable to those with lactose-intolerant stomachs. For Grand Tourists it had an even more practical appeal. The cheese had served as sustenance for pilgrimages to Rome; longevity and ease of storage were paramount. Grand Tourists, like their pilgrim forbears, appreciated the value of a hard cheese that could last the entire leg of the journey and was easy to share; they would keep chunks in their carriage and chip away at it en route. Having bought two kilos of 36-month-old organic PR, that's exactly what I did on our Grand Tour bus.

There are some 900 small Parmesan factories scattered around the Po valley and up into the foothills of the Apennines served by tens of thousands of dairy farms.

Following in the footsteps of Palladio in **Vicenza**

Vicenza is the city of Palladio, whose subsequent influence on classical architecture throughout the world – the Palladian style - was due to one British Grand Tourist: Inigo Jones.

Although my first golden destination was Venice, I always intended to return to Vicenza, an extraordinary city that I first visited twenty years ago. It is the city of one man, Andrea Palladio, an apprentice mason turned architect-cum-archaeologist who assiduously read the *Ten Books of Architecture* by the Roman Vitruvius; who travelled, measured and copied ancient temples; who decided, alone, to revive the principles of classical architecture in their purest form, and who discovered in the process that classicism is not so much a style as a set of principles and a kit of parts, an immensely flexible vocabulary that can be tuned to any building type.

The son of a miller, Palladio was born in 1508 in Padua as Andrea di Pietro della Gondola. At thirteen he became an apprentice to the stone-carver Bartolomeo Cavazza before moving to Vicenza in 1524. Though he earned a living sculpting capitals, mouldings and cornices, he gives an indication of the extent of his early ambition in his own *Four Books of Architecture* (*I Quattro Libri dell'Architettura*) when he writes: 'Guided by natural inclination, I gave myself up in my most early years to the study of architecture, and as it was always my opinion, that the ancient Romans…vastly excelled all those who have been since their time, I proposed to myself Vitruvius for my master and guide.'

In 1538, he came to the attention of Count Giangiorgio Trissino – writer, humanist, member of Vicenza's nobility and man on a mission to revive the

Andrea Palladio, the mason turned architect-cum-archaeologist who revived the principles of classical architecture, giving Vicenza an outstanding architectural legacy and, ultimately, influencing the revival of classicism throughout the Western world.

architecture and culture of the ancient world for the good of humankind. Trissino named his new protégé 'Palladio' (after Pallas Athena, the patron goddess of the arts) and took him on extensive travels in Veneto and to Rome, where he studied ancient monuments and the work of the great architects of the early sixteenth century, Falconetto, Sansovino, Serlio and Giulio Romano. What an extraordinary opportunity for that young man.

Under Trissino's patronage, Palladio started to fashion a career as architect to the Vicenzan élite. He was awarded the title of architect in 1540, and he enjoyed commissions in and around Vicenza, firstly for villas and then within the city, producing elegant, dense-looking *palazzi*, like Palazzo Thiene, set into the existing street façades. In 1549 Palladio secured his position as architect to the aristocracy with the commission to reconstruct the down-at-heel Palazzo della Ragione, or the Basilica, on the Piazza dei Signori.

A Gothic building reclothed with a classical skin, the Basilica marks an attempt to bestow Renaissance clarity and purity on a medieval city. Some twenty years later, when Palladio came to design the Loggia del Capitaniato (1565–71) on the other side of the piazza, his style had become rather more elaborate. The two dramatic façades face each other across the public square, testament to the evolution of a magnificent career.

Palladio's early work in Vincenza included elegant, dense-looking *palazzi* like the Palazzo Thiene, set into the existing street façade.

This page and overleaf
Attempting to decipher the design of Palladio's Palazzo della Ragione with the aid of a giant model from the Palladian Institute in the public square. The rhythm of the façade brings to mind Goethe's famous description of 'architecture as frozen music'. He said of Palladio's Basilica: 'How hard he worked at that. How the tangible presence of his creations makes us forget that we are being hypnotized!' British architects took inspiration from the way Palladio clothed this Gothic building within a classical skin.

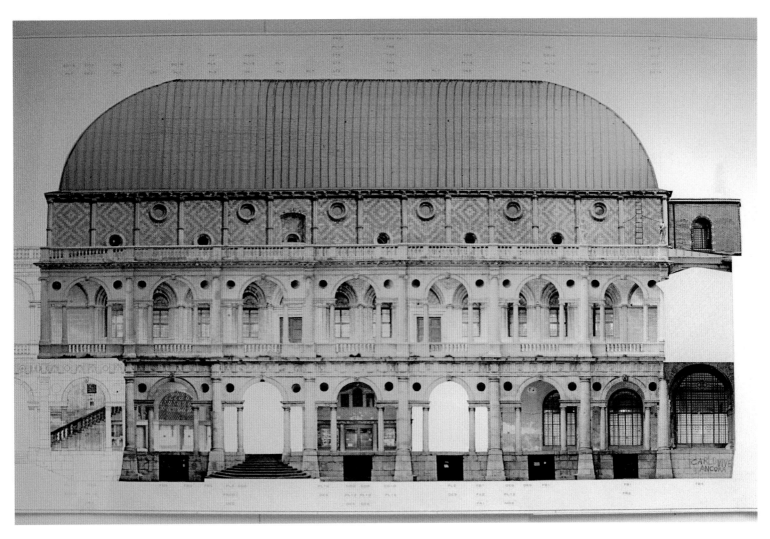

Admiring the Loggia del Capitaniato from the roof terrace of the Palazzo della Ragione, or the Basilica. This is architecture as drama: two façades having a face-off across a public square. But it is also an encapsulation of the evolution of Palladio's work. While the Basilica is still clearly a Renaissance work, the Loggia del Capitaniato, built some twenty years later, heralds the arrival of the baroque.

In his final commission, the Teatro Olimpico, which opened in 1585, five years after his death, Palladio set out to recreate the many Roman theatres he had studied over the years.

After Trissino's death in 1550 Palladio acquired new patrons, the Barbaro brothers, and developed a new client base among the Venetian nobility – eventually becoming Surveyor of Works, or chief architect, to the Republic of Venice. But he returned to Vicenza in 1579 armed with the accumulated wisdom of a lifetime's study of the architecture of ancient Rome. So it was perhaps inevitable that in 1580 the Olympian society in Vicenza commissioned him to build a new theatre, the Teatro Olimpico. Although he set out to recreate the many Roman theatres that he had studied over the years, Palladio never got to realize his vision. He died in 1580 and his great rival Vicenzo Scamozzi finished the project, complete with an elaborate trompe-l'oeil stage set, five years later. The theatre opened in 1585 with a production of Sophocles' *Oedipus Rex*. But Scamozzi's hand in this building

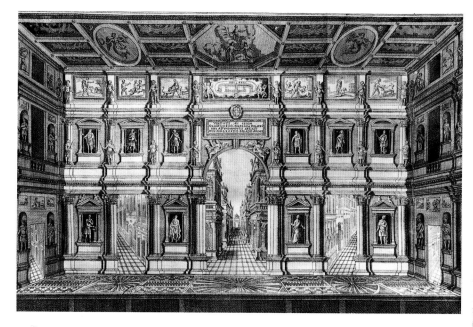

doesn't upset me. I find the exuberant passion for the Roman classical style that Palladio promoted so overwhelming and the finished building so powerful that I can gladly spend a whole day gawping at it. Inigo Jones found this building so important that he returned to it. He must have felt at home in the classical fantasies of its stage sets, machinery, lighting and architectural detailing.

It's odd, however, that the Italians have never really got Palladio. He worked in the provinces, and his approach was historical at a time when Italian architecture was becoming increasingly mannerist and jaunty. He would have remained on the fringes were it not for Inigo Jones, who, we must remember, travelled at a time when Italy was only just opening up to the British after fifty years of occupation by the Spanish. Jones described his 1613–14 Italian Grand Tour as 'the most momentous' event of his life. It was arguably the most significant Grand Tour ever undertaken, not only because of the impetus it gave to Jones' burgeoning career as a classical architect, but also because his travelling companions, the Earl and Countess of Arundel, were England's pre-eminent patrons and collectors of antiquities and art.

With a local stonemason as his guide: Jones explored Vicenza and studied Palladio's buildings first hand. By recording, comparing and annotating them he was able to decipher the grids, shapes and patterns which constitute the language of classical architecture. Such was his fascination with the master that he even copied Palladio's signature so he too could sign his drawings *à la Palladio*. Jones praised the 'admirable discretion' of the Palazzo Thiene, noting that 'being slender the pillar answers the height of the place and the addition of bozzi [rough-cut rustication] answers to the strength and rustic of the rest'. He made sketches of its

Teatro Olimpico's trompe-l'oeil stage set, designed by Palladio's great rival Vicenzo Scamozzi, marks the introduction of perspective views into Renaissance theatre. This is classical architecture as spectacle and grand display.

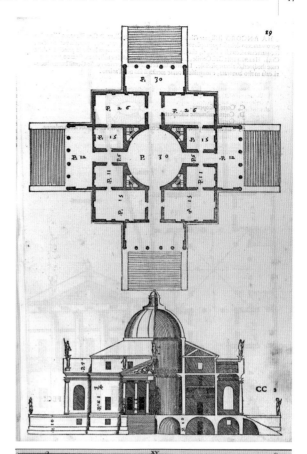

La Rotonda, Palladio's attempt to revive classical architecture in its purest form. At the time of Jones' visit to Vicenza, the roof was unfinished – there was simply a huge hole in the middle of the villa where Scamozzi, Palladio's pupil and greatest rival, would later build the dome.

entrance hall in his copy of Palladio's *Quattro Libri*, believing that entrances were key to success in design and commenting that 'The entrances are varied according to the greatness of the houses, as I observed at Vicenza, where are the best I ever saw.' He was delighted when a workman pointed out a pillar which he claimed had been carved by Palladio's own hand.

Jones also explored and recorded Palladio's urban palaces, drawing on Palazzo Barbaran and Palazzo Iseppo Porto as models when he came to design the Banqueting House on London's Whitehall. Built in 1622 to replace an earlier building which had been destroyed by fire, this was one of Britain's first classical buildings and is generally deemed to be Jones' greatest achievement. I think it remains one of Britain's finest buildings; it is easy these days to ignore because so many buildings are now designed in that same style, but the Banqueting House was the first and it has the primal energy that comes with being the first.

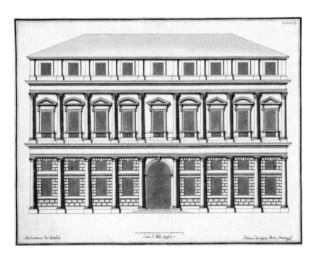

Palladio's city palace, Palazzo Barbaran, 1569–1570 (below), was a key influence in Inigo Jones' designs for the Banqueting House in Whitehall, built in 1622 (above). Generally deemed to be Jones' greatest work, the Banqueting House was one of England's first classical buildings, but its red-brick neighbours are a far cry from the rational classical streetscape Jones so admired.

Jones also marvelled at the Villa Rotonda, Palladio's attempt to revive classical architecture in its purest form, though at the time of Jones' visit its purity was somewhat compromised by the huge hole in the roof where the dome was yet to be built. Scamozzi, who had also been Palladio's pupil and who met Jones in Vicenza (and sold his entire stock of Palladio's drawings to Jones' travelling companion, the Duke of Arundel) would later build the dome. And so Scamozzi must have been able to tell Jones how he finished Palladio's theatre as well, how his own design respected but also perhaps improved on some of Palladio's wishes.

Scamozzi and Jones would have perhaps enjoyed a hearty conversation about how you don't need to fit theatre sets with glass windows, chimneys and gutters; that you could build scenery as abstract architectural confection, as a proscenium to other worlds. Then there was the delicious notion of proper architecture as a setting for pretend architecture, for spectacle and grand display. Jones' own theatre designs certainly changed after his second visit to Italy, utilizing more machinery and perspective tricks. In the Teatro Olimpico he must have felt his own career – as theatre designer, architect and champion of Palladio's peculiarly purist classicism – utterly vindicated. And although he built precious little in Britain (the Queen's House at Greenwich is his other great extant building, though much changed), and his beloved Palladio was not to be taken up for another hundred years when Lord Burlington and Colen Campbell instigated the true Georgian Palladian revival, he continued to design in Palladian style. He would never build a Corinthian-pillared street or neighbourhood in London, but he could do so in the theatre. He produced sheaves of drawings of idealized buildings and settings and by around 1620 was designing sets of extraordinary elaborateness, probably on a scale with the permanent setting at the Teatro Olimpico. This was the classical world, as defined in Rome, interpreted by Palladio and reinterpreted by Jones. In England. Just think what we missed.

Perhaps it was Jones' sense of theatricality that drew him to Palladio's façadism – the way for example that Palladio made a decent living building large country farmhouses with working farms attached before sticking an Ionic portico on the front and calling them villas (truth to tell, Palladio designed very functional interiors too). Perhaps he related to the fact that Palladio's career was hampered by cultural resistance. Both were 'slow-burners'. Palladio eventually succeeded Jacopo Sansovino as the Surveyor of Works in Venice, but only late in his career. Perhaps Jones, a maverick like Palladio, was drawn to the Italian's nerdy archaeological enthusiasms. Jones annotated his copy of Palladio's *I Quattro Libri dell'Architettura* and visited many of Palladio's referenced ancient remains, travelling as far south as Naples in 1614 to make three visits to the Temple of Castor and Pollux. In any case, Jones got Palladio. He got the flexibility of the system that Palladio was reviving and promoting. He got the theatricality of the style.

But, as with Palladio in Italy, nobody in England got Jones. He designed a great deal, but built very little. His deputies in the Surveyors' Office continued to build houses and functionary buildings in a style that was closer to Elizabethan English mannerism than anything like Jones' revolutionary classicism. His Banqueting House, when finished, was surrounded by red-brick twiddly Tudor buildings. Besides, nobody in Britain was building palaces in the turbulent early seventeenth century, just the odd gatehouse here and there. It was only in the next century that Jones' collection of drawings and the influence of Palladio began to be celebrated as the appropriate architectural style for the Georgian age. Palladio's theatre and urban palaces were the beginning of a style that has shaped every dense city centre in our country, that exploded and expanded in Britain for 200 years and which has given us almost every high-street bank and grand country house and civic building since. We have everything to thank both Palladio and Jones for.

Overleaf Palladianism didn't take off in Britain until a hundred years after Inigo Jones' death when architects such as Lord Burlington and Colen Campbell instigated the Georgian Palladian revival. Holkham Hall in Norfolk, built between 1734 and 1764 by Lord Burlington's protégé William Kent, was based on Palladio's unbuilt Villa Mocenigo. Kent's client, Thomas Coke, had acquired an appreciation of classical art and architecture on his own Grand Tour.

Life in a Palladian villa in the **Veneto**

Working farmhouses and administrative centres for lucrative estates, the villas of the Veneto were generally large, practical boxes with grand façades attached.

Beyond the confines of the city of Vicenza lay the flat and fertile lands that were the breadbowl (and rice paddy) of the Venetian Republic. Here, Palladio played to the pretensions of wealthy landowners with a new building type – something that would flatter their sense of patrician responsibility. He built his wealthy clientele a whole series of villas that might have come from ancient Rome.

This new breed of client was emerging from the decline of Venice's position as an international superpower. As its empire diminished, Venice – for the first time in history – looked to its hinterland, rather than to the sea, as a source of potential prosperity and power, and hit on the idea of subsidizing its once wealthy merchants to transform the wetlands around the city into agricultural land.

And boy did it work. This new breed of rural entrepreneurs rose to the challenge with aplomb, hastily reinventing themselves as landowners drawing on their trading expertise to import potatoes, tomatoes and maize from the Americas and rice from the East, fuelling an agricultural revolution – and a whole new social class.

The new farming élite deserted their Venetian palaces for new villas in the countryside from which they could administer their lucrative estates. Loath to forgo the convivial company that city life could afford, they built country quarters with sufficient space to accommodate like-minded guests. And they took their families with them too: it was cheaper to move the family to the farm than to deliver foodstuffs to the city. Villas would house extended families of forty or so

Palladio's villas were in a different league from typical villas of the time – but not quite as grand as he would have us believe. Imaginary wings and arcades find their way into Palladio's drawings of his work, perhaps in a bid to impress would-be clients. Quattro Libri was, first and foremost, a marketing brochure for Palladio's work.

people – the pure, quiet temples that we see today would have been full of visitors, bustle and noise.

Eager to assert their authority over this now bountiful landscape, they knocked down their medieval *castelli*, replacing them with working homes fit for the modern age. But the villas they had built were simple rectangular boxes, little more than fortified manor houses. A new architecture was required to express their authority and wealth.

Villa Pisani

The Pisani family belonged to this flourishing farming élite. Having purchased titles – as counts and hereditary vicars of Bagnolo – they commissioned Palladio to design a villa which would act as the administration centre for their vast estates but also proclaim their elevated status and ultra-refined tastes. The commission marked a step change in Palladio's client base. Whereas his previous patrons had been primarily Vicentine, the rich and powerful Pisani brothers provided an

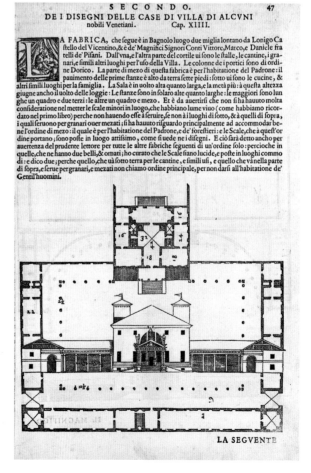

Above The great T-shaped central hall is barrel-vaulted like ancient bath buildings and rich in decoration and natural light – a radical departure from the modest halls of pre-Palladian villas, which tended to have flat ceilings and wooden beams.

Left Drawing of Villa Pisani from Palladio's *I Quattro Libri dell'Architettura*; living accommodation, stables and dovecotes are accommodated within a unified design.

entrée to the Venetian aristocracy; their influential relatives Daniel Barbaro and Zorzi Cornaro were both to become future clients.

But it also marked a turning point in Palladio's architecture. Villa Pisani, built between 1542 and 1545, was designed shortly after Palladio visited Rome – and I think it shows. The villa is raised on a high basement – like a Roman temple – with the kitchen in the basement and the granaries in the roof. The pediment is a clear nod to the architecture of the Ancients – this is the first of Palladio's domestic

Like a Roman temple, Villa Pisani rises on a high basement, which emphasizes the building and conceals the service areas. Here, for the first time, Palladio adorned a domestic dwelling with a temple front, a device which would reappear repeatedly in Palladio's work and – over time – all over Britain.

My sketch of the Villa Pisani.

buildings to have a temple front. The form of ancient thermal bath buildings is recreated in the great T-shaped barrel-vaulted hall lit by a typical Roman semi-circular 'thermal' window.

Drawing on the 'ideal' measurements of ancient Roman architecture, pinched in the main from Vitruvius' book, he brought dwelling areas, servant space and farm buildings into a coherent rational form; a harmonious composition of perfectly proportioned spaces expressed at different scales and nearly always symmetrical in plan. What Palladio succeeded in creating was a proper villa; a distinctive building type uniting the ideals of grand classic architecture with the practical requirements of the local clientele.

Self-promotion

Villa Pisani was followed by a string of villa commissions creating a landscape littered with neo-classical essays in elegant perfection, a body of work which was to have a profound influence on domestic architecture throughout the Western world. Given their remote location, they might have remained little known were it not for an audacious – and magnificent – exercise in self-publicity:

The real treat for me was not just the tourist visit but experiencing what it might be like to actually live in my 'perfect house', for owners and servants alike.

I Quattro Libri dell'Architettura, published in 1570. Ostensibly a pattern-book of classical architecture (and plenty of architects had published those), it doubled as a stunning compendium of Palladio's work.

The book was a publishing triumph. It was translated into every major European language, ensuring his Veneto villas a place on the itinerary of many a Grand Tour. The more observant visitors would have discovered that some of Palladio's villas were not as ornate as the architect would have us believe. Actually, even the most dim-witted visitor would figure that something was up. Most of the measured drawings which adorned the pages of *Quattro Libri* were enriched with imaginary arcades and wings and giant-size statuary. Palladio built one kind of building and then revisited it in his books to portray the kind of building that perhaps he enjoyed working on (just a few of his villas were built to such complexity) and wanted people to commission. He was also, perhaps, inventing an 'architecture of the mind': something that would become an important concept to the archaeological architects, like Piranesi, of the eighteenth century.

Inigo Jones would have known Villa Pisani from *Quattro Libri*, but he also saw it in the flesh, stopping off to marvel at – and measure – the masterful command of form and mass. Returning to England to assume the position of Surveyor of Works to the king, Jones was to champion a new style of court building based on the authority of antique precedent; surviving drawings for the Queen's House at Greenwich (1616–35) suggest that he saw Palladio's villas as the appropriate precedent for an architecture of refined regal restraint. I certainly felt flattered and pampered by Villa Pisani when I stayed there for one night with its current owners, who have done a great deal to restore the villa to its former working order. Its rooms are generous but not enormous and have high ceilings allowing you to feel tall and composed. Above all, the windows are large so that every space is luminously lit, something which satisfies a very twenty-first-century obsession. And that symmetrical ground plan is always evident thanks to the enormous central void of the hallway which, as in all of Palladio's villas, runs front to back. You can see through the entire house. The villa remains a flexible and civilized place to live.

A century or so later the Palladian villa, as interpreted by Jones, was to become the blueprint for what we think of as the classic English country house. Stately homes such as Houghton Hall were built to classical proportions, their grand porticos and spreading wings asserting authority over a landscape of Arcadian delights. And English Palladianism had its own diffusion range. City planning projects such as those in Bath and Edinburgh's New Town condensed a lavish Palladian scale to suit the requirements – and the budget – of high-density mixed-use urban life, proof positive of Palladio's adage that the proportions and language of classical architecture can adapt to any building type at any scale.

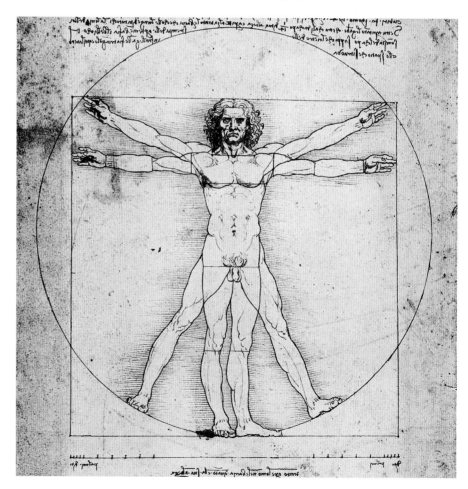

Palladian proportions are based on Vitruvian/ancient Roman measurements derived from 'ideal' human proportions. The foot is one sixth of his total height, elbow to fingertips a quarter of total height, and so on. In truth, Palladio was so gifted in laying out space, many of the proportions of his buildings seem to have been organized by intuition. He even breaks his own rules, but only by five or ten per cent. My own measurements of Villa Pisani suggest the rooms there are 'approximations' of his ideal proportions.

Above Inigo Jones, who passed by Villa Pisani and stopped off to take its measurements, developed the Palladian villa in the Queen's House, Greenwich 1616–1635, commissioned by Queen Anne. The building now houses part of the National Maritime Museum.

Left Designed for British Prime Minister Sir Horace Walpole between 1722 and 1735, Houghton Hall in Norfolk represents the appropriation of Palladianism by the British élite.

The spectacle, illusion – and debauchery – that is **Venice**

A celebrated marvel of the age, a city of façades and masks, Grand Tourists visited for pleasure first, and for architecture and art second.

I have mixed feelings visiting Venice these days. The city has become a sort of floating Disneyland, many of its houses lying empty as the permanent population has now fled to the mainland. Cheap flights and a permanent carnival atmosphere now ensure the streets are full of visitors intent on partying round the clock, full of each other and full of booze. And the upside? The thing that draws me back to Venice is not the light or the architecture or the canals but the very superficiality of the place which at once keeps the city alive and has been its undoing. It has, for five centuries, been a fascinating place of masks and façadism. Like Genoa, Venice was also a model for British sea power, a Republic and, to all intents and purposes, a democracy, with an economy centred on trade. But as early as the sixteenth century it had also turned itself into the pleasure dome of Europe. Grand Tourists came for pleasure, sex, gambling. Debauchery first, architecture and art second.

If modern Venice seems more like a theme park than a powerful city state that's because it has always played a game of double bluff. Just as its citizens doll themselves up in absurd period costume and masks to lech, gamble and drink their way through the Carnival for two weeks in February each year, so the city itself is all about show, rarely revealing its current character. Its architecture is like scenery, presenting only the façades of buildings. Its canals are not only arteries but also its auditorium from where its visiting audience (some 30,000 Brits at one single point living in the city in the eighteenth century) gasp at the marvels

Venice today is crumbling a little with age. But in the seventeenth and eighteenth centuries it was the most beautiful city on earth. It must have been astonishing to view this incredible city for the very first time.

of stage management, never privy to the backstage view of the façades, nor the engineering which is holding the place up.

Venice is a structural miracle; an apparently floating city that is a product of technical ingenuity and deliberate design. Early settlers found security camping on small islands in the lagoon that were natural defences. Over, perhaps hundreds of years, they enlarged these silt islands, rebuilding their perimeters with stones or wooden piles that would harden and petrify in the salt water. In the middle of the island they would dig a pit and line it with clay and then perhaps cover it with slabs to form a cistern for rainwater. And then rudimentary buildings would appear around the cistern, with sloping roofs to channel more rainwater to the centre. Eventually the island might grow so close to a neighbouring island that a bridge would be built.

And that, according to Venetian engineers I've talked to, is how Venice grew. The canals are the remains of the watercourses between the islands. Each 'island' still has a square and still has a cistern. The buildings are all of them still supported on dozens of petrified wooden stakes or piles, driven into the island's silt. And all of it remains

relatively stable. Venice is not suddenly sinking. The silt is still hard and compacted under the weight of the city above (Venetian engineers call it 'constipated' silt and still compress it with weights as part of the construction process today). Instead, as I was able to see in a series of photographs of paintings shown to me by one engineer, the sea has been steadily rising in the lagoon for hundreds of years. Now, ironically, giant concrete defences are being built to keep the water out of the lagoon.

I say that it is relatively stable because the perimeters of these islands are under threat. Whereas for centuries engineers would dredge the canals to prevent them silting up, now, thanks to the thousands of propellers driving river taxis and boats galore, the silt is kept in permanent suspension in the water. Venice is now losing its silt too quickly .

So it is not such a bad thing that its buildings are unencumbered with heavy overhanging porches, balconies and porticoes. In fact it's a deliberate tactic. As Matteo Negro, my engineering guide, explained, Venetian *palazzi* are constructed with minimal weight on the outside walls. All the loads of the structure are carried to the centre of the building, onto core walls and core wooden piles that are well away from the perimeter of the island. Not only that, but the delicate Gothic tracery for which the Doge's Palace, for example, is famous, is a structural necessity; it's a wall with holes in it to make it lighter.

Canaletto understood the importance of illusion in Venice. In his eighteenth-century views of London he deliberately extended the river and turned it into St Mark's Basin, populated it with gilded barges and ranged his Thames-side buildings like Venetian palaces. He was providing the take-home for British tourists — not just a memento of their trip but a reinterpretation of it on home soil.

Venetian *palazzi* were – and still are – terraced confections jostling for elbow room on the Grand Canal, squeezed and primped. Their façades are rich in surface decoration but decidedly two-dimensional: an elegant latticework of windows, tiny balconies and perforated screens.

And, I was told, there is one final characteristic of Venetian buildings that contradicts every way we build in Britain. The perimeter walls aren't locked together with cornerstones; they float independently of each other. And they lean in. Every one of them, to stop them falling into the canals. Armed with this new view of how to put up a building, it is not difficult to see why Venetian buildings are so two-dimensional, so decorated and so frothy-looking. They have to be. The entire city is a collection of theatre-set flats leaning up against each other, a piece of historic scenography crumbling slightly with age.

This theatricality has always been one of Venice's visual trump cards. The other trick it pulls off is that it appears to float (whereas of course, it's pretty solidly built on those silt islands). From the sixteenth century onwards, the English nurtured the view that Venice could be seen as a miniature reflection of the gilded isle that was Albion. Both were powerful maritime nations. Both depended on trade, both were run with parliaments answering to a sovereign authority; Venice was extremely rare in being a Republic – a model that classically-educated travellers could appreciate. Just as Elizabeth, Gloriana, had been married to her people, so the Doge was married to the Sea.

Below Early eighteenth-century oil painting by Gabriele Bella of the parade of the courtesans on the Rio della Sensa. Venetian courtesans were encouraged to display their wares quite openly in a bid to combat homosexuality. They were a formidable force in the city, wielding financial and political power.

Above Developed in the early sixteenth century and especially popular among Venetian women, the high-platformed shoe called the *chopine* was designed to protect the foot from irregularly paved and wet or muddy streets. The *chopine* also served a symbolic function: the higher the shoe, the higher status of the wearer. The tallest were twenty inches high.

Previous pages Venetian houses occupy a unique place in architectural history – they sit directly in the water and their front doors are accessed by boat. Larger houses had a sort of portico so that boats could moor up inside the house itself.

Above *Carnival* by the Venetian artist Giovanni Battista Tiepolo (1696–1770). Head-to-toe disguise was viewed as an excuse to shed inhibitions and decorum. Grand Tourists flocked to Venice at carnival time to indulge in Bacchanalean excess.

Opposite Looking up at the dome of Il Redentore. Having taken a vow of poverty the monks were in no position to embellish or 'improve' their church. It's interior remains *exactly* how Palladio planned it: a perfect dream-like essay in over-layered classicism.

And by the eighteenth century, Canaletto was playing to this perception. He understood the importance of illusion in Venice. His eighteenth-century views of London show an extended river Thames morphing into St Mark's Basin populated with gilded barges and overlooked by Thames-side buildings ranged like Venetian palaces; a tailor-made souvenir for the British Tourist – not just a memento of the city, but a reinterpretation of Venice on British soil. In reality of course, the two waterfronts were worlds apart. Venice has such visual integrity. London's sixteenth-century Thames-side palaces evolved over several generations as ramshackle collections of buildings often arranged around a yard – more medieval country farm than stately home. Meanwhile, their Venetian equivalents were terraced confections jostling for elbow room on the Grand Canal, squeezed and primped. Just as London – or any British town – outgrew its city walls over a thousand years ago and subsequently sprawled, connecting villages, infilling here and there, leaving patches of rough ground, commons, dirt tracks and grazing paddocks between its magnificent and not so magnificent buildings, Venice was all architecture, all man-made. No hills or trees; not a dirt track in the place.

And what is this city of theatre, fakery and masque, of leaning buildings and a fondness for the superficial? It is a brilliant, sparkling testament to the ingenuity and accretive labours of humankind. It reveals our inner desire for decoration and fantasy. And it has been in the business of revealing those desires – plus a few others – for five centuries.

Disease and debauchery

For every desire, there is a baser appetite. For every indulgence there is a bodily function and Venice amply represents the less appealing underside of life. Gibbon (he of *The Decline and Fall*) said that Venice provokes some moments of astonishment and some days of disgust. Venice was variously described by visitors as 'a stinkpot, charged with the very virus of hell', 'more noisome than a pigstye' and 'cursed by nauseous air'. The dirt and stench was overwhelming – the shit, piss, cooked food and dead animals were not collected by night soil men but dumped in the canal to be hopefully swept out to sea or collected by inland farmers for fertilizer. But to most British tourists the *real* source of astonishment was the air of moral abandonment and casual depravity.

In 1358 the Great Council of Venice declared prostitution to be 'absolutely indispensable to the world' and in 1596 Antonio Barzaghi published a guidebook to the courtesans of Venice complete with prices and addresses. Thomas Coryat

put the number of courtesans there in the early seventeenth century at 20,000, 'whereof many are esteemed so loose, that they are said to open their quivers to every arrow. Courtesans, of these there are whole streets full and they receive all-comers. These dress in the gayest colours with their breasts open and their faces all bedaubed with paint, standing by dozens by the doors and windows to invite their customers.' Fearing that Venice was heading into moral disrepute due to a climb in homosexual preference, the city built bridges with gaps, so men could look up, when passing beneath the bridges, and see up women's skirts.

For Grand Tourists, sex was part of the plan. This was about training to be a good lover for marriage back home. From the fifteenth century onwards, travellers returned with reports of the number and beauty of Venice's courtesans – in his comedy *Humour Out of Breath*, the dramatist John Day (1574–1640) called Venice 'the best flesh-shambles in Italy'. During nine days in the mid-sixteenth century the scholar Roger Ascham, private tutor to Queen Elizabeth I, claimed to have found 'more libertie to sinne, than ever I heard tell of in our noble city of London in 9 year'. And in 1712 Charles Baldwyn observed that 'The whole city may well be termed the brothel house of Europe.' While staying in Venice Byron boasted of having slept with different women on 200 consecutive nights.

The opportunities for debauchery were never greater than at Carnival time, when visitors flocked to the city to dress up in costumes and masks and indulge in Bacchanalean excess. Thomas Nugent, in his 1749 guidebook *Grand Tour*, observed: 'They make a sort of universal change in their habits, customs and laws, forget all marks of distinction, care, and business, and resign themselves up to joy and liberty, frequently attended with folly and great disorders.' Disguise meant anyone could be anyone and do anything: boy on boy on girl on aristocrat on nun on pauper on priest... you name it. As Nugent rather more delicately put it 'a man may take upon himself what character he pleases, so he be qualified to act the part he assumes.'

Although Venice's military dominance had waned by the eighteenth century, its past glories were commemorated in spectacular style. Canaletto's painting, *The Bucintoro at Molo on Ascension Day*, depicts a celebration of a naval victory over Dalmatia on Ascension Day, AD 998. During the event the Doge, on his golden barge, threw a ring into the Lido, as a symbol of the marriage between Venice and the Sea.

Purity and proportion

Across the water, however, there lies another Venice. An almost Puritan architecture: not baroque, not frilly Gothic, but clean, classical, monumental, almost in defiance against the diseased city of spectacle and trickery.

When Palladio became the protégé of the Venetian prelate Daniele Barbaro, he would already have been aware of the structural strictures placed on architects working in Venice – that city of decorated façades rather than the solid sculptural purity that Palladio was intent on. He never built within the city of Venice itself and probably would have found its limitations frustrating, but at least he was able to build across the water – outside the formal city limits – on the long, narrow strip of land known as the Giudecca. If Palladio never got to realize his vision of classical purity in Venice's streets and squares, he made up for it in his two churches, Il Redentore and San Giorgio Maggiore, which look out at Venice across the water, preening their pristine, white monumental façades, pointing towards

The pristine façades of Palladio's churches, Il Redentore (left) and San Giorgio Maggiore (above), watch Venice across the water. Clean, classical and monumental, their purity seems to stand in defiance of the city's culture of trickery and spectacle.

an English baroque style that was to emerge after the Great Fire of London in the work of Hawksmoor, Vanbrugh and Wren.

Despite the opulence of the interiors of his *palazzi* and villas, Palladio frowned on superstitious decoration in his churches, preferring the perfect proportions and unadorned simplicity of purer classical forms. Here he was able to create the idealized classical urban space he was never able to realize in Venice's public realm – in a language Inigo Jones was to recreate in countless designs for stage sets and which, though Jones' influence lay largely dormant for most of the later seventeenth century, would in time inform the design of countless buildings and streets throughout Britain and the Western world.

In search of the domes and sights of **Florence** – birthplace of the Italian Renaissance

Money generated in Florence, once one of the great
financial centres of the world, paid for art, poetry and
philosophy – with an emphasis on man, not God,
as the centre of the universe.

Florence, Firenze, the flowering city, may be the cradle of all that is noble and cultured in the Western world, but only because it was one of the world's great capitalist cities. Its early successes were built on trade, of foodstuffs, fine cloth and crafted goods. Money management followed. By the fourteenth century Florence was like a latter-day City of London, bent on centralizing power in a few bourgeois banking institutions. The cash generated there paid for art, poetry and philosophy – with a new emphasis: God was no longer being celebrated as the centre of the universe. Man was usurping that position. The intellectual independence that came with commercial success, the time for thought that a post-agricultural society provided, the refinements of urban life and sophisticated pursuits led thinkers to consider man such a noble and advanced creature that he needed celebrating.

Dante wrote his *Divina Commedia* here, parodying his fellow Florentines. Giotto populated his frescoes with realistic people. The Greek philosopher Protagoras had said that 'Man is the measure of all things', but in the early fifteenth century the architect-author Leon Battista Alberti really spelt that out, saying: 'To you is given a body more beautiful than other animals, to you power of various and apt movements, to you most sharp and delicate senses, to you wit, reason, memory like an immortal God.'

From around 1400 the city fathers began to invest in culture and *studia humanitatis* on behalf of their republic, but all this learning and erudition led, visibly, to rather modest works. To the eighteenth-century traveller, much of Florence's art and architecture would have seemed quite insignificant. The Medici-Riccardi chapel, decorated by Benozzo Gozzoli, was a dazzling 'who's who' of mid-fifteenth-century Tuscany, but was hardly on an epic scale. It was a tiny jewel box of a room. Giotto's much earlier frescoes were startling for their time but crude by Georgian standards. With their delicate details, the Ospedale degli Innocenti and the Pazzi Chapel, both by Brunelleschi, were undoubtedly charming, but not as robust and glorious as Palladio's Roman façades.

Above Giotto's fresco cycles in the Bardi and Peruzzi chapels in Santa Croce were realistic for their time but Grand Tourists would have found them crude by Georgian standards.

Below Brunelleschi introduced classical detailing to Florence with his design for the Foundling Hospital, the Ospedale degli Innocenti.

Gay Florence

The Grand Tourist came to Florence for other pleasures. He came to look at sculptures and paintings but also to find company – and the place to do that was the court of the legendary British consul, Sir Horace Mann. Ostensibly in Florence to spy on Bonnie Prince Charlie and his supporters, who had set up residence in the

city, Mann entertained visiting Englishmen at his home, Casa Manetti, in the Via Santo Spirito – where he also enjoyed liaisons with a series of Italian gigolos. For many Grand Tourists the gigolos were Florence's main attraction. Having held the world's first gay pride march – a protest in 1494 against the Office of the Night, the body responsible for investigating charges of sodomy – the city was known for its sexual tolerance. Sodomy between older men and younger boys was an established part of male culture. Men frequently didn't marry until they were forty and young boys were often inveigled into passive, remunerated, friendships with them.

Renaissance men

But no Grand Tourist could fail to be amazed by one building in Florence – one towering structure that dwarfs all others and still dominates the city – the dome of the cathedral. The Duomo Santa Maria del Fiore (St Mary of the Flower) was begun in the thirteenth century by city fathers who ordered the construction of a vast octagonal drum above the nave crossing, ready to take a dome. At the time they were confident that someone would develop the technology to span the huge hole in the roof, but by 1400 nobody had – until Filippo Brunelleschi stepped up to the challenge.

A trained goldsmith, Brunelleschi was part-architect and part-engineer, designing – among other things – fortifications, machinery and ships. He was perhaps the first true 'Renaissance man' – a polymath. He read Vitruvius and, with the Ospedale degli Innocenti, introduced classical detailing to Florence. And in the 1390s, with the artist Donatello, he had been on a Grand Tour of his own: to measure, climb and investigate the ruins of Rome, long before the study of antiquity became a popular pursuit.

His dome, built between 1439 and 1445, was constructed without scaffolding. It had to be. The octagonal drum on which it sits is just too high. Brunelleschi didn't using centring either – the practice of building arches on timber formers and allowing the mortar to set before removing the wooden supports. Instead, he raised the dome slowly and equally from all sides, using the wide and generous drum walls as a platform. The brickwork was laid in a herringbone pattern, allowing for an ingenious self-supporting brick matrix. Meanwhile, a system of wires and strings allowed the progress of construction to be measured and checked. By laying several wires across the void it was easy to see from the cathedral floor just where the centrepoint lay. An assistant lying on their back could then check and mark the inward progress of the walls. Further wires were then strung from the top of the drum up the inside of the dome walls to determine the correct radius of each rib (octagonal corner of the dome) as it rose.

Brunelleschi's system was unknown until very recently. My guide to the dome, Massimo Ricci, has spent his entire adult life figuring out how the thing was built and has constructed his own ten-metre-diameter brick construction model to help unravel the secrets of its construction. His conclusions have been so detailed that when conservators recently removed plasterwork from the inside surface of the dome, Massimo was able to successfully predict the location of hidden eyes and hooks that would have carried the wires. When the plaster came off, there they were.

It may seem odd that Brunelleschi's construction methods have remained so obscure for so long. But the fifteenth century was an age when architects, builders and artists kept their secrets. Brunelleschi recorded the details of the dome's construction in a complex code which itself would not be deciphered for another 200 years. According to Massimo he lay traps and visual deceptions in the structure, deliberately faking the direction of some of the brickwork so as to confound subsequent generations of engineers. But British visitors – especially architects – flocked to Florence, not just to marvel at the dome's gargantuan proportions but to glean what information they could.

It is still the largest masonry dome ever built, and it was the first major dome to be constructed as an outer dome resting on an inner one, linked by a series of ribs, rings and spandrels which are all extremely visible to anybody prepared to climb the steps and explore between the shells. For shells they are. A stone arched bridge can more or less, at its most minimal, be as thick as just one thirtieth of its length. A dome, because it is a three-dimensional self-bracing structure, like a half-spherical jigsaw, can get away with a thickness just one two-hundredth of its diameter. You can make a model bridge with a slice of melon, minus the

Brunelleschi's gargantuan, iconic dome looms over the side streets of Florence.

The architect Massimo Ricci, who has spent the last thirty years trying to unlock the secrets of Brunelleschi's dome, gives me a behind-the-scenes tour of the Duomo – and a picnic on the roof. Signor Ricci is less than impressed at my attempts to create a model of the dome with my melon. His criticism? 'A melon is round! The dome is not......'

Opposite page below Two photographs show the internal passageways between the inner and outer skin of the dome and the herringbone brickwork which allowed the dome to be self-supporting as it rose.

pips. You can make a model dome with just the melon skin. I did with Massimo. The Duomo's dome was an inspiration. Its elegant rib structure – hidden from general view by the outer skin, demonstrated how to stop a dome from bursting (its most prevalent tendency): Brunelleschi solved this extra problem by inserting iron and stone 'chains' around the structure. At every turn, with every new challenge, he devised a brand new solution to make it work. It delivered an engineering masterpiece which was to inspire both Michelangelo's St Peter's and Sir Christopher Wren's St Paul's.

Like Brunelleschi, Christopher Wren was a multi-disciplinary genius. Born about 250 years later, he was a gifted draughtsman and mathematician, who by the time he was designing St Paul's in his thirties had already been Savillian Professor of Astronomy at Oxford (he considered, as did many, architecture to be a branch of scientific practice). Surprisingly, he never visited Florence – in fact he never went on the Grand Tour at all. But Wren was surrounded by scholars and aristocrats who had been to Italy and seen the ancient wonders of the world, and he designed St Paul's on the basis of models which others brought back; people such as the fifth Earl of Exeter, who made three extensive Italian tours and accumulated a vast collection of contemporary baroque paintings, ranging from intensely devotional images to

Taglio del medesimo Tempio fatto sulla Linea IK della Figura II.

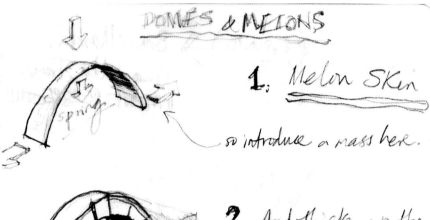

DOMES & MELONS

1. Melon Skin

so introduce a mass here.

2. And thicken up the arch.

3. Whole melon skin. very strong. But impossible to construct

4. A series of Arches that spread!

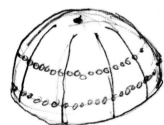

5. A series of chains that hold the arches together.

Overleaf *The Last Judgement*, a fresco by Giorgio Vasari and Federico Zuccari on the interior of the Duomo.

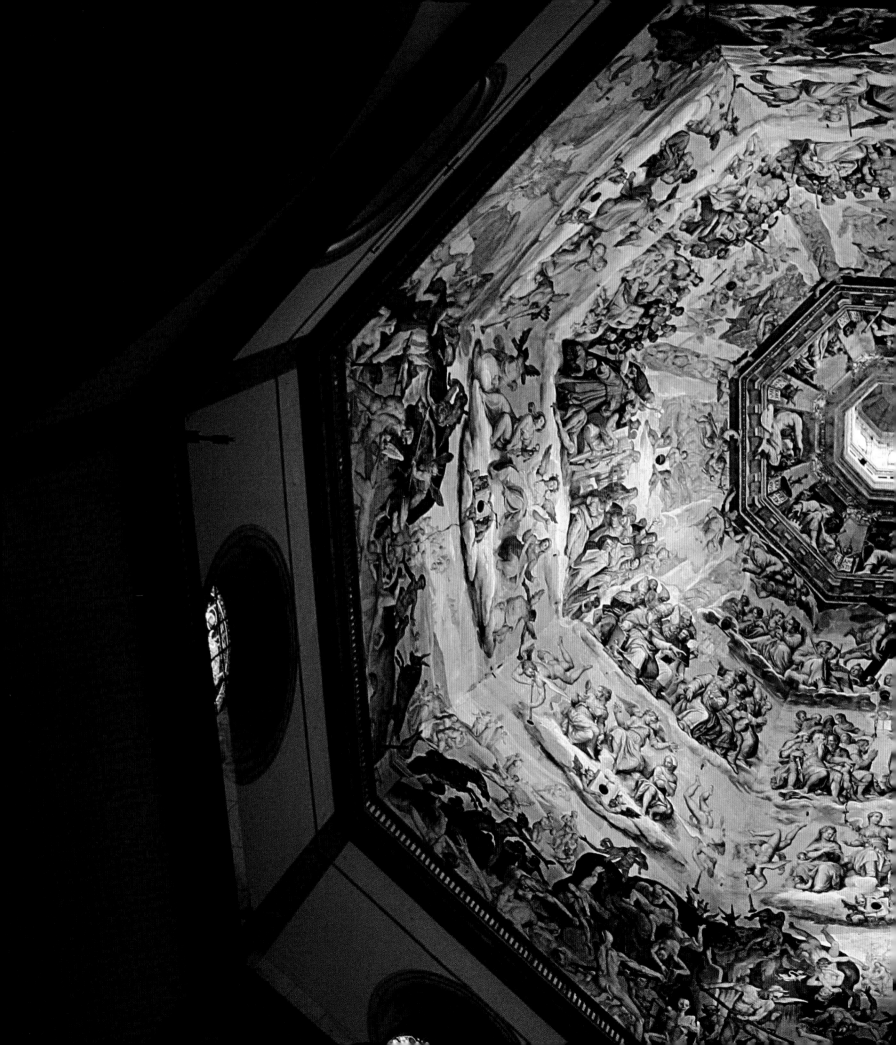

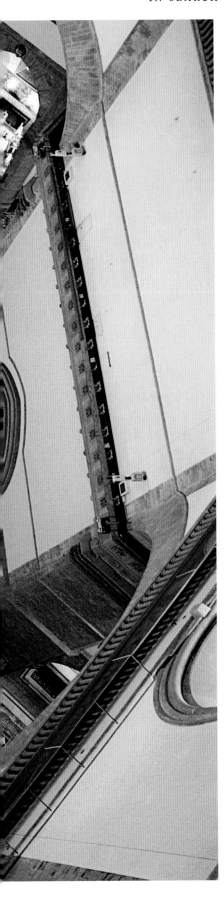

The vertiginous view down from inside the dome.

highly erotic mythologies. In addition, Wren could draw on his own mathematical knowledge. He was an assiduous model maker, using papier maché and card. As a co-founder of the Royal Society, he would have been involved in its discussions in 1640 on 'The Correct Shape for Arches', and would have been familiar with the work of another co-founder, his great friend Robert Hooke, which established the principle that a parabola, or more correctly, catenary arch, is inherently more stable than a semicircular arch or dome. Hold a chain or length of string between two points of the same height and you have a catenary arch. Draw it, turn it upside down and that is the perfect shape for an arch or dome. It's not semi-circular but you'll find that, in the cross-section of any built dome or arch, this is where the loading is carried down through the structure.

Wren used catenary arches in his designs for St Paul's. Perhaps, just as importantly, he kept in his office a beautifully detailed scale drawing of two foreign domes shown side-by-side for comparison – those of the cathedral in Florence and St Peter's in Rome. Wren took Brunelleschi and Michelangelo for his inspiration, both in their aesthetics and their engineering solutions.

And Wren was interested in Brunelleschi and Michelangelo as men. It's been suggested that Wren adopted architecture as a career because it offered him the chance of high profile public acclaim. He wanted fame. Brunelleschi's dome was not just a technological wonder; its size and height make it visible for miles, even from surrounding cities. It wasn't a celestial symbol but a very earthly one, asserting the pre-eminence of Florence – and it introduced a Roman scale. It wasn't a medieval spire pointing to God but a giant dome beaming a message to the Heavens, saying: 'Look what I can do. See how I can defy your laws of gravity and build my own celestial globe.' Whereas the seventeenth- or eighteenth-century aristocrat might have sneered at the Pazzi Chapel, he would have been dumbstruck by the way the dome dominates the city, punctures the sky and asserts both man and the man himself, Brunelleschi. This would have been compelling for Wren.

The first town planner

Brunelleschi had also, unwittingly, become one of the first town planners, another idea that appealed to Wren. He is credited – amongst others – with having invented single-point perspective, allowing for the accurate rendition of public spaces and buildings. It's said that he laid out the Cathedral Square in Florence and then painted a picture of it using his new technique before inviting guests to

look through a pinprick he made in the painting, placed exactly on the 'horizon' of the painting, and examining the picture in a mirror. The result, supposedly, was uncannily three-dimensional. He also lobbied to have the area in front of San Lorenzo Church, for example, cleared to form a piazza. Though medieval cathedrals dominated their cities, nobody since the Romans had allowed urban form to be determined by anything other than military needs. But now Brunelleschi, it seems, was demanding the creation of public space (to admire his buildings admittedly) and was able to accurately render them before they came into existence, using these newly formed perspective tricks derived from painting. Michelangelo was to adopt similar mathematical techniques to lay out the Campidoglio in Rome, methods that would have chimed with the mathematician Wren.

Celebrity and power

It is perhaps easy to see why Wren might have been so beguiled by the celebrity culture of architecture in the Italian Renaissance. Over the course of the fifteenth century the humanist view of man as the centre of the universe gave way to a culture dominated by personality and fame. By the summer of 1665, when Wren briefly met the fashionable sculptor Gian Lorenzo Bernini in Paris, that cult was at its height. Constantly surrounded by a throng of admirers, Bernini was a true celebrity, while Wren, for all his achievements, was just another visitor in a long line. Bernini played the role of diva with aplomb, loftily exhorting his host King Louis to 'Let no-one speak to me of anything that is small,' and blithely bitching about the king's taste, houses, courtiers – and wife.

Adrian Tinniswood explores the possibilities of a meeting between Wren and Bernini in his book *His Invention So Fertile*, citing how the two great men would have concurred on so many levels. Wren, seeing himself as a Vitruvian, famously remarked that 'Architecture aims at Eternity' out of respect for the time-honoured truth and geometry of classicism. Bernini, too, saw 'a thousand faults in St Peter's and none in the Pantheon'. Both believed in mathematical truths and geometry as underlying the natural world. Both were giants in their field. But their meeting was probably extremely brief and dull. Bernini was interstellar, an international diva sculptor, a Pavarotti of stone. Wren was an ex-academic with pretensions to architecture, a wannabe with a building in Oxford to his name.

Wren had some mountain to climb. If Bernini represented the apotheosis of celebrity culture, Brunelleschi was a pioneer of city branding. As the first Renaissance building to rival the epic architecture of the ancient world, the

Duomo's superdome gave Florence a giant personality. Almost a century later, as the fifteenth century evolved from an age of realism and humanism to one of super-realism and heroism, it was Michelangelo who defined the essence of contemporary Florence. Firstly with his statue of David – a High-Renaissance hero on a truly colossal scale – and then with the Medici Chapel. Michelangelo's work, occurring a century after Brunelleschi's, doesn't so much celebrate man as create from him a new species, half-God.

From Superdome to Superman

Commissioned at the end of the 1400s by the Medici family, the wealthiest and most powerful of the wealthy bankers who climbed out of the Florence power-cradle to become rulers and popes, the Medici Chapel is extraordinary, both architecturally and as a statement of power. Here Michelangelo makes free with the classical orders – stretching, chopping and redesigning them to achieve maximum sculptural effect. The void in this chapel, the space, is as carefully crafted as the blind niches, sculptures and columns. Michelangelo saw himself as a sculptor rather than an architect, and this is a building that can only have been conceived by a sculptor with a highly developed spatial mind, as though he'd started with a 5,000-ton block of rock and hollowed out this room. But it's clear that, despite his strenuous denials, he was a gifted avant-garde architect and an extraordinary interior designer too, albeit something of a maverick.

Heaven knows what the puritanical Palladio would have made of this creative interpretation of the classical orders. Suffice to say there's nothing of Michelangelo in Palladio's *Quattro Libri*. And Michelangelo preceded Palladio by fifty years. I think Palladio must have visited and been unnerved by the audacious rule-breaking of this place and its negative energy. It is a dome of sorts, a flattened dish of a ceiling that looks like it might spin off like a Frisbee, the place hums so much. It certainly bears no relation to the dome that Michelangelo was to design for St Peter's in Rome.

Perhaps the most outrageous thing about this chapel is that Michelangelo depicts the two Medici Popes not as the gouty old men they really were but as handsome Roman princes – objects of veneration in their own temple, almost Gods themselves. Where Brunelleschi's dome was a symbol of Church and State, the Medici dome was all about the enforcement of a dynasty and unabashed personal power. And there are many that have found and continue to find such personal architectural statements offensive.

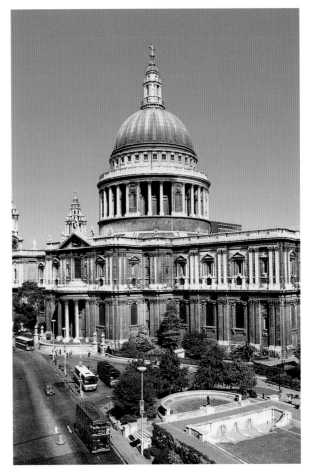

Top opposite Michelangelo's David defined the essence of contemporary Florence: a High-Renaissance hero on a truly colossal scale.

Centre and bottom opposite Sketching the Florence Baptistry using two-point perspective. Built between 1059 and 1128, the Baptistry is one of the oldest buildings in the city.

Above St Paul's Cathedral: a Duomo on home turf.

Travelling through Tuscany

Grand Tourists followed the old Roman roads and pilgrimage routes to Rome, breaking the journey to seek respite from the fatigues and ills of their trip. The Tuscan air was deemed to be particularly healthy and most British visitors fell ill at some point on their Tour. Some, including the English Romantic poet John Keats, embarked on the Tour in poor health, hopeful that the balmy climate would have a restorative effect. Things didn't always go to plan: Keats' tuberculosis deteriorated en route and he died in Rome in 1821. Others picked up ailments on their travels. Tourists were often described as having 'nervous breakdowns', 'tempers' or 'fits', but were as likely to be suffering from the effects of sunstroke, sexual promiscuity, poorly-prepared food or copious quantities of booze.

The locals drank wine instead of water, ostensibly on health grounds: it was deemed to improve the blood, aid digestion, calm the intellect, enliven the spirit and expel wind – if drunk in moderation. British Grand Tourists, who *loved* Tuscan wine, shocked the Italians with the sheer volume of their alcohol consumption with many, including Pitt the Younger and the playwright Richard Sheridan, routinely drinking six bottles of wine a day. This heroic level of consumption was fuelled by the Florentine tradition of noblemen selling wine from their Tuscan estates

The Fiat 500 has to be *the* way to travel through Italy. I was occasionally allowed to borrow one when I was eighteen and working on a farm in Tuscany. Boys would congratulate you when you drove it. Girls would stop and admire it….

Overleaf A view over the rolling hills of the Tuscan countryside from our hotel.

directly to passing trade, and by the British ritual which required every person at the table to make a toast, after which the assembled company downed an entire glass of wine. Excessive Grand Tour drinking was deemed rather dashing and something of a badge of honour. When a group of Grand Tourists established the London dining club the Dilettanti in 1734 Horace Walpole observed 'the nominal qualification is having been in Italy, and the real one, being drunk', adding that its leaders, Lord Middlesex and Francis Dashwood, 'were seldom sober the whole time they were in Italy'.

The small medieval village of Bagno Vignoni, conveniently located on the fifteenth-century pilgrimage road to Rome and blessed with hot spring waters in an ancient Roman bath, was a particular draw. In Renaissance Italy 'taking the waters' was deemed an appropriately gentlemanly pursuit. The romantic notion of the rustic retreat and the fact that men and women bathed together, wearing little, if any, covering, added an additional *frisson*. More importantly, the sulphuric waters, from natural springs, were thought to cure arthritis, rheumatism, broken bones – and much else besides. I went for a swim in the ancient Roman Bath with all manner of minor ailments and emerged fully healthy, twenty years younger with enlarged pectorals and all my own teeth back. It was a miracle.

A miracle indeed. The reputation of the place seduced the Marquis de Sade to Bagno Vignoni, probably in a bid to cure his gonorrhoea. Boswell and Charles Dickens both recharged their batteries here on the way to Rome. And many a Pope, Medici and Grand Tourist drank diuretic cures to heal their gout. Variously described as a disease that 'kept good company' and the 'disease of kings', gout, aggravated by the excessive consumption of alcohol, purines, offal and red meat, was the ubiquitous ailment amongst those of high rank. (Petrarch, the fourteenth-century Italian Renaissance poet, saw gout as a disease with a moral purpose, designed to discourage frivolities and excess). The Medicis, in particular, were notorious gout-sufferers. Cosimo de'Medici died from the ailment in 1464 while his son Piero de'Medici earned the unenviable nickname Pieri il Goltoso – Piero the Gouty – before he too died of the disease. Piero's son, Lorenzo the Magnificent, also suffered from gout and visited Bagno Vignoni in search of a cure.

But most Grand Tourists were simply smelly. After weeks spent travelling in a crowded carriage in the summer heat the baths must have been a godsend. This was before the days of deodorant, and opportunities to bathe en route were few and far between. Travellers had to resort to wiping their armpits, groin and teeth with a coarse linen cloth doused in vinegar – the antiseptic of yesteryear. Imagine the joy, the delight, the absolute rapture, of indulging in a good old soak.

Bagno Vignoni, with its ancient Roman baths, has attracted tourists for centuries. The economy of this tiny Tuscan village is still dependent on its natural springs. And people still believe in their powers – they still come, not simply for pleasure, but to be cured of ill-health.

The classical wonders of **Rome** – and indulging baser appetites

While half the Grand Tourists in eighteenth-century Rome were busy making diary entries, recording ruins and copying and designing, the rest were drinking, gambling and whoring.

The great historical gateway to Rome from the north – the one that the late-seventeenth-century Grand Tourist would have entered – was the Porta del Popolo. Immediately inside the city walls was a vast square, the Piazza del Popolo, with a pair of twin-domed churches at its end, where three great streets fanned out into the distance. No visitor would have been in doubt that this place meant business, order and control; not of the Medicis or any other banker or merchant but of arguably the most powerful man on earth – the pope.

Pope Sixtus V and his architect Carlo Fontana had laid out streets and boulevards in the 1580s. Popes could do this. They could order people out of their houses and then tear them down to make way for a new square, fountain or obelisk. St Peter's was newly complete and in the 1660s Bernini would add his weird and powerful ovoid piazza. In every direction, views terminated in grand buildings, open-air staircases and statuary. Rome was a paradise of extraordinary architecture and public spaces – a heady mixture of brand-new infrastructure and buildings and extraordinary ancient ruins.

But Rome had only just emerged from a thousand years of obscurity, dirt and dereliction. The architectural historian John Summerson once called it the architectural 'compost heap' of Renaissance Italy – a city that had collapsed. In the 1530s just 30,000 people inhabited a city built for a million, leaving space aplenty for the popes to implement their extraordinary vision for a new Papal City on an epic scale.

And so a new city emerged, with grand avenues and huge public squares, whose fountains overflowed with water brought in on remodelled Roman aqueducts. Fontana organized the installation of dozens of obelisks: religious symbols to their original owners, the Egyptians, and subsequently employed by the Romans as emblems of power they were now town planning devices, points of focus and interest in avenues and squares. The long Piazza Navona was built on the site of an ancient race track, which you can easily imagine when you stand there now. There were three large fountains and by plugging the drains the whole pavement could be flooded, making the piazza into an enormous pond in which the churches and palaces all around were mirrored. Aristocrats amused themselves by driving through the water while lesser mortals stood by and watched the fun.

In the Piazza del Campidoglio on top of the Capitoline Hill – the historical centre of Rome – Michelangelo had refaced or redesigned buildings and made a virtue of their odd arrangement. What he did indoors at the Medici Chapel in Florence he did here outdoors – he built a 3-D dream world, controlling the space with sculptural shapes and an intricate paving design in the form of a

Piazza Navona Under Water painted by Pannini in 1756. Built over the walls of the Stadium of Emperor Domitian (the entrance to which can still be seen) it has always been a site of public spectacle. Here the fashionable aristocrats of eighteenth-century Rome amuse themselves driving their carriages through axle-deep water.

twelve-pointed star. He brought every part of the piazza into play: the buildings, colonnades, steps, and the gilded bronze statue of Marcus Aurelius in the centre, from which the energy of the place seems to spring. Odd to think that, until he did this, statuary had always been placed in or next to buildings and loggias. In the early sixteenth century Michelangelo set the tone of Rome by using statuary as a town-planning device. Fontana was merely to copy him, substituting for statues the very useful obelisks he just happened to have at his disposal.

Brunelleschi in Florence and Michelangelo and Fontana in Rome were creating a new discipline – urban design – which we now tweely call 'placemaking'. Then it was about creating a new Roman world, re-energized and interpreted for a new Papal order. And the popes could do it because there was no-one to oppose them. For the Medicis in Florence it had not been so straightforward.

And if we jump forward again to England in the 1660s, the decade that Wren met Bernini, we find that Rome's urban layout, the work of Fontana and Michelangelo, was the inspiration for Sir Christopher Wren's plans to rebuild London after the Great Fire in 1666. When you look at his plans for London you can see a direct link between what he was *trying* to do and what the popes in Rome actually did. Wren's designs were among several proposals submitted to the king after the fire. John Evelyn's own proposal bore a striking resemblance to Wren's. But in London there were too many vested interests and Wren's and everyone else's plans were scuppered.

If you want to remodel a city, a fire that destroys 13,000 buildings clearly isn't enough. You need a city which is empty, as Rome was. It also helps if you've got

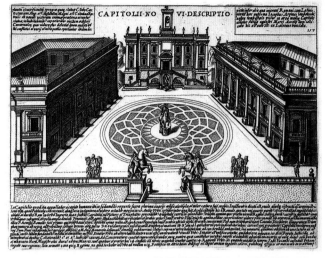

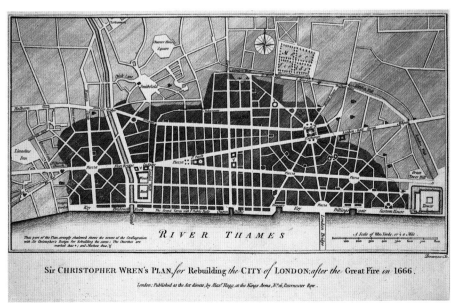

Sir CHRISTOPHER WREN's PLAN, *for* Rebuilding *the* CITY *of* LONDON: *after the* Great Fire *in* 1666.

London: Published as the Act directs, by Alex.' Hogg, at the Kings Arms, N.º 6, Paternoster Row.

Above In the Piazza del Campidoglio on top of the Capitoline Hill – the historical centre of Rome - Michelangelo built a three-dimensional dream world, controlling the space with sculptural shapes and an intricate paving design in the form of a 12-pointed star. He brought every part of the piazza into play: the buildings, colonnades, steps, and the gilded bronze statue of Marcus Aurelius in the centre, from which the energy of the place seems to spring.

Left Following the Great Fire of London Christopher Wren tried to lay out the new city following the principles of public space, wide streets, vistas and terminations that Carlo Fontana did for Pope Sixtus V in the 1580s.

Overleaf From the sixteenth century the Popes carved Rome into a succession of public piazzas, grand vistas and huge domes. What better way to see it than from above?

a despotic monarch or emperor as Paris has had in its time. Or best of all, a pope. We hardly ever got it right in Britain because our cities weren't laid out by despots – and they hadn't been laid aside to crumble for a thousand years. They were busy vital places that had grown from villages and towns and it was hard to reinvent them in any other than their sprawling form, grown as they had on principles of the free market and freehold ownership. The only real exceptions are Bath and Edinburgh – eighteenth-century model towns laid out on a truly grand scale and done so on huge speculative scales.

Rome's domes

Presiding over all this papal splendour were two magnificent epic domes – the Pantheon and St Peter's – and the tiny, but equally perfect, Tempietto. All of them control the space within them and around them and are as important as town-planning devices as they are objects in themselves and chapters in the history of

The Pantheon, the most famous dome in the world. It may be a church, but no amount of Christianizing this space can hide the fact that this is a powerful, primal, pagan building that does anything but make one feel virtuous. Dubbed the House of Devils at the height of the Grand Tour, this is a blood-raising, gigantic, mysterious place which does indeed feel as though it were created by devils, not man.

Checking that the Pantheon matches up to Palladio's exquisite drawing. At rooftop level, it's possible to admire the construction of the magnificent dome. The portico, with its massive granite columns, is an astonishing structure in its own right.

our greatest cities. Mix elements of all of these structures together and chuck in Brunelleschi's dome in Florence and you get England's most iconic church – St Paul's Cathedral. Everything in that building came from them. I mention this because in no small way my trip to Florence and Rome was underwritten by my interest in domology; in how Wren managed to build one of the most perfect early baroque buildings in the world, inspired by structures he never saw for real. So I want to dwell for a moment on those few buildings that influenced him profoundly.

Although the Pantheon, the most famous dome in the world, has been converted into a church, no amount of Christianizing it can hide the fact that it is powerful, primal, and pagan – and does anything but make one feel virtuous. It is gigantic and mysterious, like a building created by devils – and was indeed known as the House of Devils at the height of the Grand Tour. Renaissance thinkers believed it had been constructed by demons, not humans, such is its scale.

Even today, the Pantheon evokes a sublime response. You are overawed by its size and ability to diminish you and at the same time you feel ennobled in its presence. The experience is akin to standing on top of a mountain where you experience that same paradoxical sense of scale. The oculus – the hole in the Pantheon's roof – is as wide as a three-storey house is high. The floor (not the original since in the ancient world the building had several forms and floors and was restored by Emperor Hadrian) is slightly domed itself, as if to make you feel like a god yourself, standing on the surface of a global planet just a mile in diameter. The dome above you, meanwhile, is raised on a drum so that it will accommodate, exactly, a sphere to the same diameter. You feel that volume, you can sense it pressing down and into the space you stand in. After visiting the Pantheon, you need to go and lie down and then spend the rest of the day sitting in the shade drinking Prosecco.

At the opposite of the domological scale is another building known to Wren, the tiny but famous tin-pot Tempietto, built by Bramante, the first architect of St Peter's in the early sixteenth century. It has been called the most perfect building in the world. This type of circular structure with a colonnade and dome now seems so commonplace to us – think of all those country houses with a little temple in the garden, all those insurance-company buildings with something like this plonked on top. But what would the Tempietto have felt like at first, when it was such a departure from the norm? It is extraordinary to think that, when it was built in 1502, Henry VII was on the throne here and we were living in wooden houses. We had no conception of this kind of architecture, which reinterpreted the classical world in a different way and was adventurous and brave. The Tempietto took the circular temple form – found for example at the Temple of Vesta at Tivoli – compacted it, made it rhythmically tauter, added balustrading and a second projecting storey, windows, niches and a dome, breathing a completely new narrative story into the building type. It turned a temple into a miniature home, or a shrine. Bramante used the colonnade, balustrade and other circular rhythms to set the building spinning like an inverted top around its dome and the energy he infused into this little miracle was a direct inspiration for St Paul's Cathedral. I know Wren never visited Rome and so never saw this building, but I can't quite believe it because the dynamic rhythms and energies of St Paul's seem to be directly lifted from here and from no other Italian dome. For example, Bramante used sixteen columns, Wren exactly twice that number. Wren in Paris visited the domes of St Sulpice and the Sorbonne. They must have been informative, but not as inspirational as this place.

And Wren got that inspiration principally from Palladio's rudimentary book. The Tempietto was the *only* building by a contemporary architect that Palladio included in his published works. He ignores Michelangelo completely, as I've said. He includes engravings of his studies of the theatre of Marcellus and the Pantheon (both useful to Wren at various times) but reserves a special place for the Tempietto. Wren originally toyed (in one of his many versions of the St Paul's design) with miniature Tempiettos on the West façade of the cathedral, settling eventually for one giant version in the middle.

But the Tempietto also wielded enormous influence closer to home – first and foremost on Michelangelo and the greatest of all baroque monuments, St Peter's.

The tin-pot Tempietto, built by Bramante (the original architect of St Peter's in the early sixteenth century) is a shrine to St Peter and thought by some people to be the most perfect building in the world. For such a tiny structure, it has wielded enormous influence…first and foremost on Michelangelo and the dome he built down the road: St Peter's.

Michelangelo developed the design of the dome of St Peter's with the aid of an enormous model, currently kept in the Sangallo Rooms of the cathedral. The iconic dome, crowned with a tempietto, has been the centrepiece of countless paintings, including Giovanni Paolo Pannini's *Departure of the Duke de Choiseul from St Peter's* painted in 1754 (left).

The new cathedral replaced a medieval basilican church which was on the verge of collapse. The commission originally went to Bramante, who started work in 1506 on a building in the form of a Greek cross with a huge central dome, but he died in 1514 when it was far from complete. After several years of discussion and numerous changes of plan, the 72-year-old Michelangelo took over the project in 1546 with an even bolder version of Bramante's scheme – and it's this that was eventually built.

It is another double-skinned structure, inspired by Brunelleschi's engineering and not finished in Michelangelo's lifetime. It isn't even the exact shape he originally wanted, being taller and more elegant than his planned perfect hemisphere. But as the sectional model made for him demonstrates (and it still does because, as I discovered, it still exists, a five-metre-high half-cupola), it is an essay in structural elegance. Not an ounce of material is wasted or excessive; the openings, buttresses and skins are reduced to their essentials; and you can trace that catenary line down through the structure to a razor's edge width of the building's periphery. It stands up perfectly, but only just.

I suspect this is why Wren had that drawing that showed half of Brunelleschi's structure sitting on medieval walls and half of Michelangelo's balancing on the piers of St Peter's. Wren could no doubt fancifully trace the paraboloid line down through those drawings. He could pin them upside down on his wall and hold a piece of string against them and know how they defied gravity. And this knowledge led him to design St Paul's not as one dome, or two, but three: one exterior skin that follows a slightly elongated profile; one internal plastered dome above the Whispering Gallery and main crossing, a dome that is bizarrely tapered but which follows its own catenary line (and is painted with fake architecture half-pinched from the Pantheon so as to give the illusion of a hemisphere sitting on a drum); and one hidden structure in between these two domes, a perfect straight-lined cone to support the lantern. Wren figured out that to obtain the best shape for a dome supporting a heavy weight, all he had to do was to suspend a miniature heavy weight from a chain or string held at two points; in other words, he distorted a catenary line or parabola into a 'V' shape, the inversion of a cone. Wren's practical, model-making, mathematical genius was ever his salvation.

Wren's cathedral also benefits from its integrity as one building designed by one man with the minimum of interventive fuss from the Cathedral Commissioners. Despite enormous opposition to his progressive classical building, Wren knew that their meddlings would come and go over the long construction period and so was consistently reluctant to reveal too much in the way of detail on the building. He had licence from the king to change the design as he saw appropriate. In effect

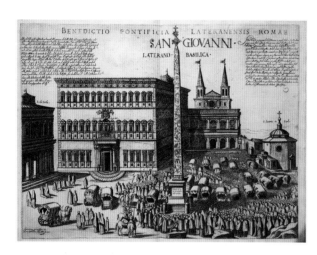

Dedication of the ancient obelisk brought to Rome in 1588 during the papacy of Sixtus V. The decision to site the obelisk in front of the Basilica di San Giovanni in Laterano was typical of the extraordinary programme of place-making which transformed Rome into a Papal city on an epic scale.

he was able to control progress by rewriting his own brief to some extent. And the result is magnificent.

St Peter's never enjoyed that integrity. It was a bastard project that passed through several architects' hands. But then, it isn't so much a building as a series of events for the faithful to experience: an embracing piazza, a raked approach to a façade, a gloomy interior, chapels galore and a magnificent blue and gold dome spinning above their heads like a spaceship. This is the theatre of Catholicism and no culture has managed to rival the pomp and the circumstance, the audacious fakery of it.

So given that in Rome the Church commissioned pretty well every new decent building, what was the British view of this popish architecture? Well, perhaps it is the excessiveness of all this gilding and marble, the heady incense and the smoke that led the British Grand Tourists of the seventeenth and eighteenth centuries, and their architects, to then look beyond the Christian architecture for something purer and cleaner, that would resonate with their own more restrained Protestant characters. From the early 1700s they started to come to Italy in pursuit of something else: something much more primitive, much more mysterious, and which they viewed as much more truthful. And that was the Rome of antiquity – the classical world.

Joining Palm Sunday Mass (taken by the Pope himself) I realize that St Peter's Square is an open-air extension of the Church: an extension of the Pope's reach. The two giant porticos are the maternal arms of the Catholic Church welcoming saints and sinners into its embrace, the façade as the shoulders and the dome as the Head. This is architecture as pure power, for Grand Tourists then – and for tourists today – this is the quintessence of Italy and Rome.

Bad tourists

While half of the Grand Tourists in the eighteenth century were busy making diary entries, recording, drawing, designing and copying, the rest were drinking, gambling and whoring. Perhaps it's what you'd come to expect from a bunch of young men on their year off and despite the best efforts of their tutors or guides – known usually as bearleaders – many remained ambivalent about Europe's cultural splendours, and instead were either dazzled by its more dubious distractions or apathetic with *ennui*.

Reports of 'bad' tourists are legion. In 1762, the fourth Duke of Gordon managed to obtain the services of Johann Winckelmann, the greatest antiquarian and most sought after guide of the age, the man who in fact invented Art History as a discipline – but refused to step out of his carriage to admire the Belvedere Pavilion at the Vatican. Which seems a trifle ungracious. Lord Baltimore, who 'wearied of everything in the world' and was pleased with nothing except St Peter's and the Apollo Belvedere, finally 'got so unbearable' that Winckelmann would have nothing more to do with him.

Winckelmann found a more appreciative audience in the radical journalist and politician John Wilkes (1725–1797), who described him as 'a gentleman of

Johann Winckelmann (above), the greatest antiquarian and most sought–after guide of the age. Grand Tourists often needed a lot of encouragement to appreciate even such famous sites as the Colosseum (right).

exquisite taste' – possibly because he pretended not to notice when Wilkes and his mistress nipped off for a shag behind a ruin during a tour of Rome.

But most young Tourists couldn't care less for the culture. In fact it was common practice for many to leave sightseeing until the final day of the trip, when the coach driver would be instructed to hare round from site to site while the tourists ticked them off in their guide-book one by one without leaving their carriages.

Imposing some order

Despite this lack of interest, even the most lackadaisical Tourist would have been expected to display some acquaintance with the orders of classical architecture; to know his Doric from his Corinthian.

Developed by the Greeks and (continuously) refined by the Romans, the orders had been codified since the Renaissance; packaged up into distinctive, neatly defined and easily digestible architectural styles in the way that a modern introduction to buildings would talk about 'modernism', 'brutalism' or 'Arts and Crafts' when in truth they form part of a continuum. But this didn't worry people like the Italian Renaissance architect Sebastiano Serlio (1475–c.1554) who, in *The Grammar of Architecture*, took inspiration from the remains of classical Roman buildings and from the written descriptions of the first century AD scholar and builder Vitruvius to redefine building styles. Where Vitruvius had endowed the different orders with personalities, Serlio went further, and suggested that each of the orders should even be ascribed a particular use.

The Doric (which in archaic Greek architecture looks almost Egyptian and is without any ornamentation but which in the Roman world had many of the go-faster accessories of later styles, things like plinths and turned capitals), which Vitruvius saw as exemplifying 'the proportion, strength and grace of a man's body', was in Serlio's view for churches dedicated to the more extroverted or macho male saints. The primitive Tuscan order (something of a concoction) was suited to fortifications and prisons, while the 'feminine slenderness' and curvy capitals of the Ionic lent itself to places of learning and more 'matronly' saints.

Serlio thought the Corinthian, which Vitruvius described as imitating 'the slight figure of a girl', was virginal in character and ought to be for the exclusive use of the Madonna. Strange, given that the orders originally belonged to a mainly pre-Christian world. But then Serlio had his opponents. Sir Henry Wotton (1568–1639), James I's famous ambassador to Venice, thought Corinthian 'lascivious' and 'decked like a wanton courtezan'.

Today, you or I can examine the virtues of any of these five Serlioid styles in almost any high street. Each style has its designated column style with the appropriate capital (top) and base/plinth (bottom) and its own entablature (horizontal beam and decorative cornice) above. Each has its own peculiar alphabet of weird decorative emblems, from daisies to cows' skulls, iron nails to bundles of reeds. When these styles were at their height in Britain, in the eighteenth century, they formed a catalogue of brands, from which you could select the 'look' that most suited your business or activity. Grand Tourists could decide for themselves from a three-dimensional catalogue when they visited the Coliseum – a textbook multi-tiered showcase with the simple Doric order at the lowest level, the feminine Ionic in the middle and the outrageous Corinthian towards the top. For aspiring classical architects, the Coliseum demonstrated one of the most sophisticated expositions of the orders. And it was in the city that represented the ancient world at its most sophisticated. A city that every week yielded a new discovery, a new unearthing.

The great Scottish architect Robert Adam, the man who really introduced Roman classicism to Britain in the 1760s, where it became known as neoclassicism, lived and worked in Rome between 1755 and 1757, convinced that 'my whole conception of architecture will become much more noble than I could ever have attained by staying in Britain.' His brother James was in Rome between 1761 and 1763, where he was inspired to design a new order – the British Order – to adorn the capitals of the portico of his supposed new parliament building in Westminster. The scheme was never built but the order, complete with lion and unicorn, thistles and roses, British crown and the collar of the Order of the Garter, was used in the gateway to Carlton House in Pall Mall.

It struck me as peculiar that an architect could be so consumed with the principles of classical architecture that he was prepared to bastardize them so much in the service of a national identity. James Adam's British order is an attempt – one of many in the eighteenth century – to identify a style of building that belonged to Britain exclusively. And he was prepared to plunder the principles of classicism to get there. I couldn't help responding with my own design for a twenty-first-century order that combines the cultural emblems of Britain now. I think my ideas are equally as ludicrous as his and for that matter not much less appropriate than a bunch of leaves, nails and cows' skulls carved out of stone. The classical orders may have survived into the modern age and we may still enjoy them, but their iconography, language and purpose, all of which were intimately tied to Greek and Roman worship, rituals and landscape, remain completely lost on us.

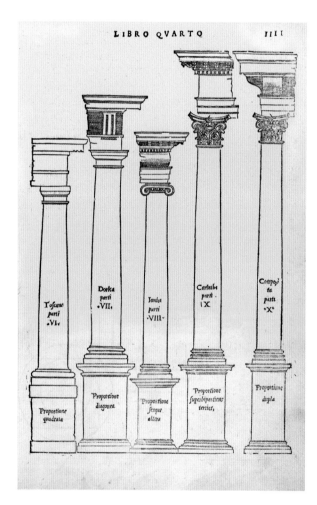

The five classical orders of architecture as set out in Serlio's *The Grammar of Architecture*.

Examples of classical detailing
seen in the buildings of
Robert and James Adam.

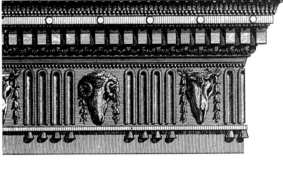

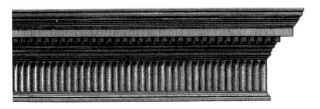

Left James Adam's design for the 'British order' for the exterior capitals for his design for a new parliament building in Westminster.

Right The McCloud order. A personal update of James Adam's 'British order'. Mine is called either 'ironic' or the 'Whatevah order'.

microphones of celebrity
the breasts of Jordan.

USB a
headphones

ringpulls.

credit card

tagner.

dildo.

Below and Right The Forum. In the Grand Tour era it would not have been the archeological site it is today, but a pastoral idyll of antique columns dotted amongst grazing cows.

Bottom The best way to see the Colosseum is to imitate the open carriage of yesteryear and jump on a scooter.

Cork models were popular with Grand Tourists both as souvenirs and objects of study. Measuring a buttress of a Roman arch behind the Theatre of Marcellus before making a tiny cork model to take home.

Condoms in the Colosseum

If the Colosseum represented the apotheosis of classical architecture, its numerous dark alleys and corners also appealed to Grand Tourists' baser appetites. The shadows were the haunt of prostitutes who could be bought for 14 paoli (about 7 shillings) a go. In 1752, the soldier and statesman Henry Seymour Conway claimed: 'There are but two things at all thought of here – love and antiquities, of which the former predominates so greatly that I think it seems to make the whole history and the whole business of this place.'

Perhaps this goes some way to explaining why Vitruvius' descriptions of the orders sexualises them. In Italy, in admiring the most refined of arts, you are never far from food, drink and lust. The eighteenth-century British traveller must have been struck by the vitality of art and architecture in Italy, its sensuality and base humanity. James Boswell, the diarist and ninth Laird of Auchinleck, justified his behaviour by referring to classical texts, boasting of having 'a girl every day' in Rome while citing: 'I remembered the rakish deeds of Horace and those other amorous Roman poets and I thought that one might well allow one's self a little indulgence in a city where there are prostitutes licensed by the Cardinal Vicar.'

Promiscuity was sanctioned not only by ancient precedent, but by the traditions already laid down by previous generations of Grand Tourists. It wasn't unknown for fathers to arrange amorous liaisons – often with their own ex-mistresses – on their sons' behalf. But it came at a cost. Venereal disease – known by a variety of names, including, unsurprisingly, 'the French disease' and 'the Italian disease' – was the scourge of the Grand Tour and protection rudimentary at best.

As early as the sixteenth century the Italian anatomist Gabriello Falloppio advocated condoms (of a sort) as protection against venereal disease. His book, *De Morbo Gallico* (1564), gave details of condoms made to his own design: linen pouches dipped in salt and herbs and tied under the foreskin with a little silk ribbon. These would no doubt have protected an amorous couple from absolutely nothing. Including pregnancy.

Linen condoms were still in use in the eighteenth century, when Casanova wore them both as protection against syphilis and 'to put the fair sex under shelter from all fear'. The linen must have been extremely robust. Over time, though, animal intestines became a more popular material. Louis XVI could afford a luxury model lined with velvet and silk and known as une *capote d'anglais* – an English raincoat. But whereas Louis had the royal condoms delivered by diplomatic bag from London, less privileged Grand Tourists struggled to maintain supplies. The first dedicated condom shop was opened in Amsterdam in the eighteenth century,

Above Casanova and friends seeing who can blow up a condom into the biggest balloon

but condoms were hard to track down in Catholic states, and particularly in Rome. Grand Tourists could stock up before the journey, buying condoms from one of two rival establishments in Mayfair, or, as a last resort, they could purchase a *Miss Jenny* en route – a hand-washed condom used by a previous owner and sold on as nearly new. Condoms, it turns out, were routinely washed and reused on account of their exorbitant cost.

Sexual healing

Unpleasant as this trade might have been, it serviced a market where the alternatives were even more unpalatable. Treatment for sexually transmitted diseases was imaginative, rather than effective. The Sicilian poet, philosopher and physician Tommaso Campailla (1668–1740) treated syphilis patients by having them sit in wooden barrels and inhale mercury infusions. Alternative treatments included rubbing sulphuric acid into the boils and pustules on the genitalia or injecting mercury up the urethra. The idea is eye-watering and yet, despite this barbarism, Italy and its universities were at the forefront of medical science. We tend to think of the Italian Renaissance as being about art and architecture, sculpture, poetry and music. But it was as much about scientific advancement and the systematic construction of cultural edifices where sciences and the arts could cohabit and interdepend. Towards the close of the fifteenth century, hospitals in Western Europe were transformed by the efforts of new, more enquiring surgeons, armed with their multi-disciplinarian Renaissance education. Anatomy became a recognised study. Dissection was performed by such masters as Leonardo da Vinci, who was known as the originator of cross-sectional anatomy – another line on what must be the ultimate Renaissance CV. From the 1600s budding scientists and doctors had flocked to Italy hungry for medical knowledge to take back home, and the acclaimed medical school at Padua became a popular stop on the Grand Tour.

The inter-related developments in medicine and science on one hand and the evolution of art on the other produced at least one curious eighteenth-century anomaly. One human being, Giovanni Battista Piranesi (1720–1778) seems to have responded to the rising discipline of anatomy by taking a thoroughly anatomical approach to buildings. He studied the structural properties of Rome's ancient ruins and thought an understanding of construction was fundamental to his art. He began his working life like a true scientist, by observation, but later moved on to the creation of anatomical experiments in architecture; the creation of fantastical interiors, studies of the guts of buildings.

NUOVO TEATRO ANATOMICO
nella Università Romana

The Enlightenment gave rise to growing curiosity about medicine and science. By the eighteenth century museums of anatomy and science were part of the tourist trail.

The darker side of architecture

When Piranesi arrived in Rome in 1740 the city was dotted with artists churning out city views for Grand Tourists to take home. But having at the tender age of twenty notched up expertise as an engineer, stonemason, architect and set designer, he was to portray the city as it had never been seen before.

He described his own work as a scholarly endeavour, saying: 'When I realised that in Rome, the majority of the ancient monuments were lying forsaken in fields or gardens, or even now serving as a quarry for new structures, I resolved to preserve their memory with the help of my engravings. I have therefore attempted to exercise the greatest possible exactitude.'

This is Piranesi talking like Leonardo in his fascination for human anatomy. At the very least, he is responding as a surveyor and his methods were certainly meticulous. Just as an artist studies the human skeleton before painting a nude, Piranesi would spend weeks living among Roman ruins, exploring the secrets of their construction, and surviving just on cold boiled rice. And this monkish existence was not without its compensations. Legend has it that he met his wife Angelica Pasquini while he was studying the ancient ruins of the Forum, and possessed her there and then – neatly combining business with pleasure at one of Rome's most venerable sites.

Many of Piranesi's survey drawings and engravings exemplify that 'greatest possible exactitude'. It's possible to compare the soil levels illustrated in his depictions of the Forum, for example, with the soil stains on the exposed buildings and triumphal arches – now at high level. I found it delightful to chart just to what point these buildings were buried before excavation and to cross-refer the soil markings on the marble with my Piranesi illustrations.

But there is that dark, imaginative side to Piranesi too, the side that we know him for. Some of his engravings are pure fantasy. Views of fictional places are distorted and light and shade exaggerated – all in the interests of drama and conveying a mood. This is of course what ruins invite you to do – to fantasize about past worlds and make a leap of imagination to fill in the gaps and 'furnish the mind'. Piranesi's genius was to capture the tension between rational observation and the romantic imagination – to combine topographical accuracy with a heroic, tragic testament to the power of Roman architecture.

His *oeuvre* found a particularly receptive audience among British visitors to Rome, who would purchase Piranesi prints to display on their walls back home. And of course his very accurate *Vedute di Roma*, a collection of engravings executed from about 1748 until the end of his life, became the ultimate holiday memento for the eighteenth-century connoisseur.

Tempio della Fortuna Virile, ora S. M.ᵃ Egizziaca
Piranesi inc.

When Piranesi first arrived in Rome in 1740, there was already an established trade in views of the city. But he took it to another level. Many of his engravings were an accurate record of the city's sites, but others had a dimension of fantasy – a romanticism which tourists enjoyed.

Opposite Like countless Grand Tourists before me, I leafed through the prints for sale on a market stall.

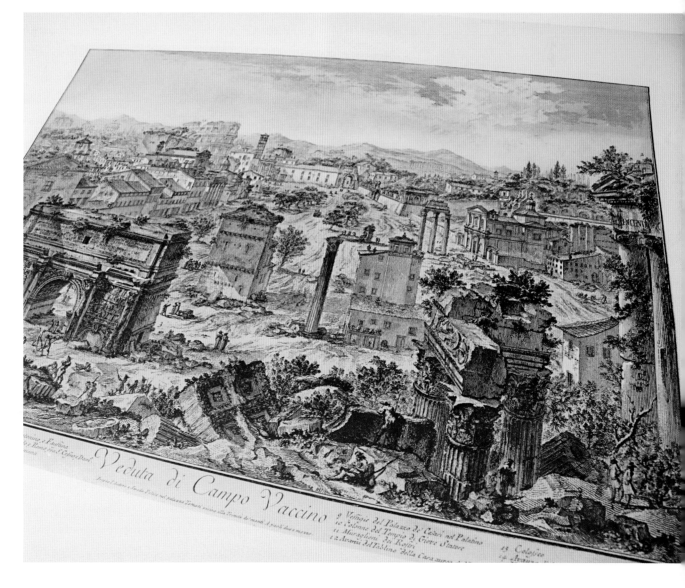

The pleasure grounds of Tivoli

One of the greatest 'Vedute' for the Grand Tourist was not in Rome itself but a short carriage drive outside the city walls, to Tivoli. Here, you could explore the substantial ruins of Hadrian's Villa and before that, chance perhaps on the Temple of Vesta, an unusual (at least to the eighteenth-century eye) circular building composed of columns.

The temple sits above the wide plain of the Campagna, beyond Rome, a plain with a rich history. It was the battleground of the ancient tribes of Latium and the Sabines, the Volscians and Etruscans. Bounded by the Alban hills to the south, with Tivoli and the Sabine hills to the east, it was also a romantic and well-publicised Grand Tour landscape – a gratifying composition of natural wonders and ancient ruins.

The temple itself is an exquisite Corinthian edifice and it seduced and inspired countless visitors. Sir John Soane adapted its architecture to create the 'Tivoli corner' of his 1793 Bank of England, while more literal imitations – including William Kent's Temple of Ancient Virtue at Stowe and Sir William Chambers' Temple of Solitude at Kew – grace the gardens of many English country houses.

Though the celebrated view of the Temple of Vesta *was* (and still is) magnificent, it might have fallen short of the Grand Tourist's expectations. While many had painted its pastoral charms, poetic licence was *de rigeur*. So it wasn't unusual to find a painting in which the temple itself was juxtaposed with the waterfall, which in fact is further downhill and a hundred metres away, with a bridge which didn't exist and with a setting sun over the domes of Rome, which could only be justifiably included if the artist were in a helicopter. Five miles away.

This wasn't 'greatest possible exactitude'. This was 'artistic licence' or 'utter fiction'. It was in fact the inspiration for a great British movement, the Picturesque. Through much of the seventeenth century, the French artist Claude Lorrain (1600–1682) had depicted fictional classical settings, usually involving some water, a temple and a group of small people, with the title 'The Queen of Sheba setting her Barque up against the Jetty of Lysistrates' or somesuch. Innocent twenty-something Brits slogged round Italy throughout the eighteenth century looking for the places where these paintings had been executed only to discover that the places didn't exist. There are plenty of pictures showing the Temple of Vesta in unlikely cohabitations with other buildings and natural features. Not something Piranesi would have respected.

And yet it produced an imaginative response that Piranesi no doubt did admire. Inspired by the paintings of Claude and aided by new-fangled technology, the

It wasn't unusual for paintings such as the one above to juxtapose the Temple of Vesta with Tivoli's famous waterfall which is, in fact, some distance away. The temple inspired numerous imitations including Mussenden Temple (opposite) in Castlerock, Northern Ireland.

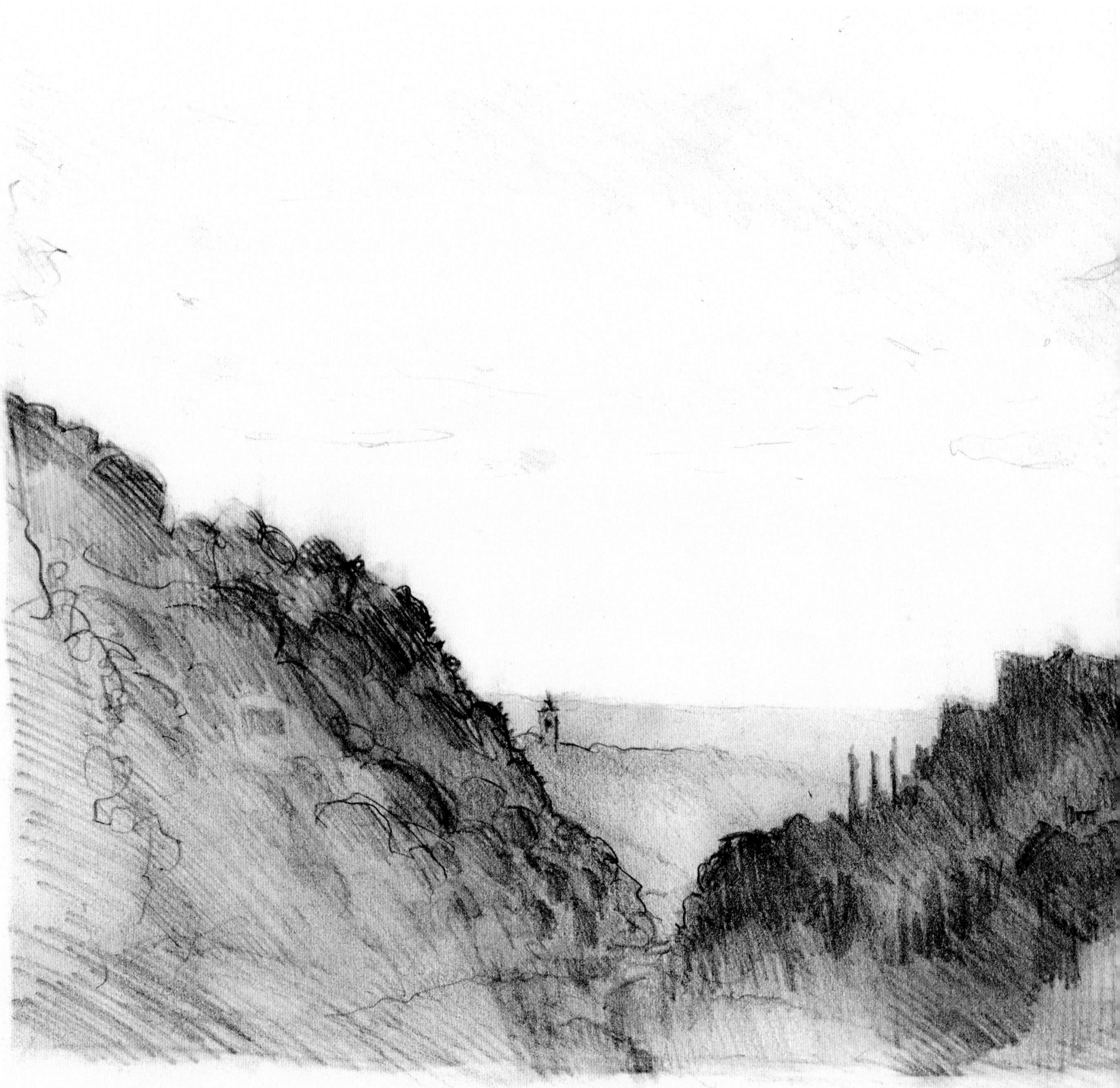

budding Georgian amateur artist could produce a passable sketch or watercolour of any landscape that would possess the same impressionistic and luminous quality of a Claude. The technology? A Claude Glass, a convex, tinted mirror designed to condense a sprawling panorama into a neat, compressed view and reduce its contrast bandwidth to extremes of light and dark. Turning your back on the landscape, you held up the mirror to appreciate the scenery as a ready-made picture – distorted, compact and neatly framed. The mirror was compact and easy to use, a drawing aid that could almost guarantee results and which simplified the interpretation of the view. It was the wide-angle lens of its time. Come to that it was the box Brownie camera of its time.

The practice of distorting scenery to create the perfect artificial image suggested something else in the young aristocratic and architectural mind: an emerging belief that man-made landscapes should be painterly as opposed to architectural. The eighteenth century saw a growing enthusiasm for this idea – a reversion from

Grand Tourists and amateur artists often made use of a Claude Glass in order to condense the view into a suitably picturesque composition. Using the same technique, I produce my own sketch of Tivoli – a particularly popular spot.

the formal geometric artifice of gardens such as those at Versailles. The *English* garden would aspire instead to the informal simplicity of the natural world. If it were possible to adapt classical settings and buildings in paint, why shouldn't it be possible to recreate not just the ancient world, but fictional ancient landscapes in our own countryside, in Britain?

It sounds absurd doesn't it? And yet , this 'picturesque' idea, of remodelling swathes of British landscape, is exactly what inspired young aristos like Henry Hoare II, the son of a wealthy banker, who returned to Wiltshire and created in the 1740s one of the most idyllic landscapes in the world on his family estate at Stourhead. Hoare – or Henry the Magnificent as he came to be known – created a 100-acre fictional paradise. He dammed the River Stour to form a great lake, directed his gardeners in the art of 'painterly' landscaping, and generally proved just how much effort was needed to get the natural look. The result? An Arcadian wonderland which could have come straight from the Claude Glass lens: life imitating art imitating life. It is still there, the first English attempt at a 3-D reproduction of a Claude painting, replete with temples, a bridge, grottoes and a lake. Every device needed for a re-enactment of any scene from classical mythology, and still today, in my view, one of the most exquisite pieces of landscape design ever carried out.

In the 1740s the banker Henry Hoare transformed the grounds at Stourhead, Wiltshire, into a scene that could have come straight from a Claude Glass.

Hadrian's Villa

If there is a comparison to make between what Hoare was trying to do in the 1740s and the Ancient world, the true similarity lies in the scale of his ambition. As Henry the Magnificent (named cheekily after Lorenzo il Magnifico, the great Medici Florentine patron) pursued the innovative and imaginative, collecting ideas from across the continent and several centuries, so he was treading in the footsteps of the great collectors and builders of the classical world. If Henry's inspiration was partly a fictional setting at Tivoli, so a very real setting just outside Tivoli was the stage on which the greatest benign Emperor of Rome, Hadrian, would build his own paradise, itself collected and re-imagineered from cultural ideas garnered from around his world.

Hadrian's Villa is perhaps the greatest rural palace of Antiquity. Built between AD 118-128 by the Emperor Hadrian, it was a dazzling assortment of thirty or more buildings on a 300-acre site, with the hills of Tivoli as a scenic backdrop. Much of the architecture was inspired by monuments elsewhere in Hadrian's vast empire, particularly in Egypt and Greece. It was constructed and staffed by thousands of slaves. The nearest equivalent we have to Hadrian's Villa is Euro Disney (or Las Vegas, given that Harold Macmillan thought Britain should play Greece to America's Rome).

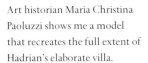

Art historian Maria Christina Paoluzzi shows me a model that recreates the full extent of Hadrian's elaborate villa.

Drawing on the writings of Pliny the Younger (c.61–112), who described the way that Roman villas embraced their natural surroundings, a succession of post-Renaissance architects envisaged Hadrian's Villa as a seamless synthesis of architecture and landscape; a dazzling procession of indoor and outdoor spaces with unexpected vistas – a confection of towers, pavilions and gardens, of fountains, nymphs and lakes. Of course, as a ruin, an abstraction, the villa gave visitors plenty of room for interpretation. Architects responded to the ruins according to their personal preoccupations; their particular classical dreams.

So, for example, Piranesi, whose signature, dated 1771, can be clearly seen in the villa's Cryptoporticum, lived here in a makeshift campsite, less concerned with imagined former glory than with the evocative decay of the ruins themselves.

Robert Adam imagined a direct lineage between the villa and the English country house. He suggested that elements of villas built in Britain by the Romans later made their way into Jacobean architecture, giving as an example the four corner towers of Syon House by the Thames at Isleworth.

To the purist Palladio, the villa's wilful eccentricity was an affront – a challenge to his belief that all Roman buildings complied with strict Vitruvian rules – but the English architect Sir John Soane was drawn to it precisely because of its eclecticism. He echoed its meandering spatial complexity in his designs for the Bank of England in London, which his associate Joseph Gandy painted (in faithful Piranesi style) as a ruin – a nod perhaps to the notion that the British Empire would suffer the same plight as Ancient Rome, but more importantly as an assertion of ruinous architecture as the more imaginative kind, one which leaves more to the viewer to reconstruct in their mind.

Robert Adam, though, found perhaps the most useful and inspirational ideas at Hadrian's Villa. Here, as at the Emperor Diocletian's Palace at Split, which he visited and recorded extensively, are the expressive ideas that he was able to import to Britain, market and promote to huge success. Ideas like the Apse, a semi-circular bay at the end of a rectangular room with a half-domed roof, like an enlarged niche if you like. Or the use of low-relief symmetrical plasterwork patterns (there are still some patches of this on some of the ceilings at Hadrian's Villa which Adam drew and recorded). Or the use of vivid colour. Adam hovered these ideas up and presented them in a new coherent style of design and decoration that we still marvel at today and associate, more than any other style of building, with the great English Country House.

Dating from AD 118-128 the complex of thirty or more buildings was composed as a dazzling procession of indoor and outdoor spaces, a seamless synthesis of architecture and landscape.

Countless Grand Tourists made the pilgrimage to Hadrian's Villa — and many made their mark on the ruins.

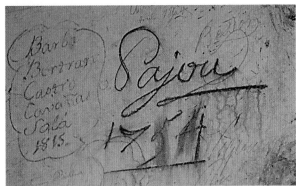

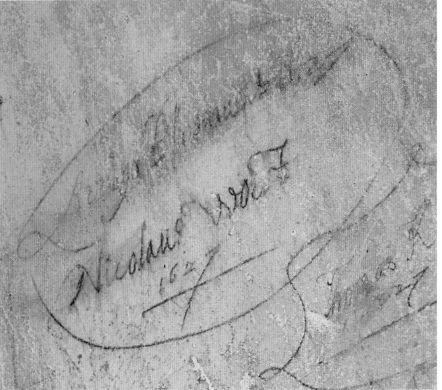

The Maritime theatre: the ruins on the island are thought to be a miniature villa where Hadrian sought refuge from the pressures of daily life. In Hadrian's day the moat was crossed with two wooden ramps, which could be easily removed to give the impression that the island was inaccessible.

As a collection of ruins, the villa allowed visitors plenty of room for interpretation, leaving architects free to visualize the original architecture according to their particular tastes.

Overleaf One of the most impressive parts of the villa is the Canopus, a long canal lined with caryatids.

To the hot south and **Naples, Vesuvius, Herculaneum** and sex at **Pompeii**

The Bay of Naples was an A-list pleasure ground
and commercial powerhouse in classical antiquity
and its sulphurous volcano and magnificent
ruins became a magnet for Grand Tourists.

The area around the Bay of Naples has been a magnet for the rich and famous since the days of Ancient Rome. It is the Hamptons of the ancient world. Julius Caesar owned a villa in the area; Cicero, the great orator and politician, owned three; Nero had his mother Agrippina murdered on the beach at Baia; Caligula built a bridge of ships between Bacoli and Pozzuoli; Tiberius ruled the Roman world from his villa in Capri.

Its status as an A-list pleasure ground was compounded by its many thermal baths – a serendipitous side effect of volcanic activity. Those at Baia, the premier vacation resort of Augustan Rome, were particularly renowned, though as much for wanton behaviour as for their curative powers. The poet Sestus Propertius was dismayed when his lover Cynthia visited Baia without him, imploring her to 'leave corrupt Baia, just as quickly as you can; those beaches will give divorces to many, beaches which were the undoing of chaste girls. Ah! May the waters of Baia perish for their crime against love!'

The area was not just a hotbed of political intrigue and pleasure, but a commercial powerhouse too. Volcanic ash from Vesuvius was so highly regarded as a building material that it was shipped across the Roman Empire (and volcanic Tufa Stone was valued for its lightness thanks to the bubbles in it) while the harbour of Pozzuoli became the largest imperial harbour for trade between Italy and Egypt.

But for eighteenth-century visitors, the big draw was Mount Vesuvius itself. Grand Tourists would hurry to Naples – and if necessary change their plans – if they heard that the volcano was about to erupt. Obligingly, it was particularly active during the Grand Tour's heyday. While there were just four documented eruptions in the seventeenth century, there were six between 1700 and 1750, five between 1751 and 1767, and eight in the 1770s. The spectacle of its fiery peak amid the beauty of the Bay of Naples chimed perfectly with the growing interest in all things natural and the fashionable fixation with the Sublime.

Edmund Burke's *Philosophical Enquiry into the Origin of our Ideas of the Sublime and Beautiful* (1757), contrasted the Sublime – uncontrollable, awe-inspiring and majestic – with Beauty – harmonious, symmetrical and soothing. This distinction, between rapture and awe, symmetry and chaos, beauty and ugliness, was to permeate thought throughout the later eighteenth and early nineteenth centuries. It helped Wordsworth crystallize his thoughts about nature, informed the poetry of Byron and Goethe and provided a platform for the Romantic movement. And it held the minds of eighteenth-century Grand Tourists who had been grappling with the strange and vast experiences they had encountered abroad. Margaret Grenville, who witnessed an eruption of Mount Vesuvius while en route to Constantinople where her husband was ambassador, wrote: 'At night it was really a glorious sight, and perfectly answered Mr Burke's idea of the Sublime.'

Mount Vesuvius was particularly active at the height of the Grand Tour. With Luigi Maisto, a vulcanologist and expert on Vesuvius, I make my way gingerly to the volcano's edge…

In time-honoured tradition
I pick up some mementos
of my visit – both artistic
and geological.

Such close proximity to sublimity had, it seems, an intoxicating effect. In 1767 the antiquarian – and first great art historian – Johann Winckelmann, and a party which included a young German baron on his Grand Tour, decided to picnic on Vesuvius the day after an eruption. When they reached the lava fields the foreigners stripped off their clothes and, naked, uncorked bottles of wine and roasted pigeons over the burning lava. I couldn't find any pigeons or lava fields and so decided not to strip off when I visited.

With its vertiginous crater, Vesuvius forms a brooding backdrop to the Bay of Naples.

Naples then and now: a maze of alleyways and unexpected finds. But the riot of colour conceals a huge amount of poverty - which perhaps explains the popularity of the public lotto.

Hostages to fortune

As you might expect from a population which has spent thousands of years at the mercy of a capricious volcano, the inhabitants of Naples were, and are, astonishingly superstitious. They trust their future to fate, to chance, to fortune – and to the public lotto.

The popularity of the lotto, with its promise of sudden wealth, has always doubtless been due to the fact that many Neapolitans lived – and still live – in abject poverty. In the eighteenth century, of a total population of 300,000 an estimated 40,000 were *lazzari* – a tight-knit class of paupers who survived on the streets, picking pockets for a living, and, according to the English poet Thomas Gray, 'relieving themselves whenever they felt the urge'.

There had been desultory attempts to temper the civic lust for gambling with some sort of moral code. In 1581 the viceroy banned Naples' citizens from placing unseemly bets on the life of the pope. And in 1688, after a particularly serious earthquake, the public lotto was suspended as an act of repentance on the off chance that natural disaster might be a punishment for misdeeds. But fourteen years of abstinence were deemed quite enough and business resumed as usual in 1712.

As to the weekly draw, contemporary accounts describe huge crowds excitedly arriving in the central square to hear the winning numbers read out. Joining the throng and observing the colourful behaviour was a popular Grand Tour pursuit. Visitors thought the fiery peak of Vesuvius and ever-present threat of danger were in fact key to understanding the Neapolitan character. In his *Italian Journey*, Goethe wrote: 'it strikes me that these earthly paradises are precisely the places where volcanoes burst forth in hellish fury and have for centuries terrified and driven to despair the people who live there and enjoy these regions,' adding: 'it is a strange experience for me to be in a society where everyone does nothing but enjoy himself.'

In his guidebook *The Grand Tour* (1749), Thomas Nugent described Naples as 'a paradise inhabited by devils, the people being reckoned, ignorant, lazy, unconstant and more addicted to venereal pleasures than the other inhabitants of Italy.' That said, the volcano, or perhaps just the heat, appears to have had an aphrodisiac effect on visitors too. James Boswell confessed that: 'During my stay at Naples, I was truly libertine. I ran after girls without restraint. My blood was inflamed by the burning climate, and my passions were violent.'

By the 1630s Neapolitans were known across Italy as macaroni-eaters and they had begun to export the product. Macaroni became the symbol of Naples, and the word used to describe affected, camply-dressed Grand Tourists when they returned to Britain.

Learning to make macaroni in
the traditional way.

I'm invited to the famous neoclassical Villa Lucia, overlooking the Bay of Naples. Built as a replica of a Herculaneum villa, it is now owned by a lady senator in Berlusconi's party. The evening's entertainment includes reenacting Emma Hamilton's notorious 'Attitudes'.

Scholarship and scandal

But Vesuvius was also the source of more scholarly pursuits. Sir William Hamilton (1730–1803), British envoy in Naples from 1764 to 1801, was obsessed with the volcano, climbing it some sixty times and engaging in serious scientific research. From his rented farmhouse at the foot of the mountain he monitored the volcano's activity, collecting rock samples and sulphur and sending regular reports to the Royal Society in London.

Sir William is credited as the founder of modern vulcanology, establishing for instance that Pompeii was buried not by Vesuvius but by its neighbour Monte Somma. A spectacularly illustrated collection of his reports on vulcanology, *Campi Phlegraei* (1776), became a standard purchase for the Grand Tourist. When he successfully predicted two eruptions, his credibility was assured.

But Sir William's reputation as a scholar was overshadowed by his colourful private life. Widowed in 1782, he went on to marry Emma – a former 'hostess' turned artist's muse and one-time mistress of his nephew, Charles Francis Greville. This charming but penniless young aristo had needed to get her off his hands to make an advantageous marriage of his own, so had packed her off to Naples and his solitary uncle.

Delighted with his beautiful trophy wife, Sir William invited Grand Tourists to watch Emma performing 'Attitudes' – re-enactments of classical poses and scenes culled from his collection of antique vases. While modern scholars have interpreted the performances as an attempt to recreate Roman pantomime – a serious art form in the Ancient world – contemporary accounts suggest something closer to soft porn. That said, Emma's poses were static, clothed and tastefully presented in a 'frame' as if she were a three dimensional painting. It might seem a trifle arch and pretentious, but we decided to re-enact the poses with a local Italian model and a diaphanous Greek dress plus accoutrements such as tambourine and veil. The results, I have to say, were both beautiful and slightly erotic: full of classical poise, the kind you find in sculptures in the British Museum but infused with the pulse of flesh and blood. Like watching statuary come to life. If this was pantomime I'd volunteer to don tights and slap my thigh any day.

Perhaps the sensuality of our event (we had a small audience even) was coloured by what we knew of Emma. The *frisson* surrounding the Hamilton marriage blossomed into full-blown scandal when she – as Lady Hamilton – embarked on a very public affair with Lord Nelson, apparently with Sir William's blessing. The three later lived together openly in Britain with Emma giving birth to Nelson's daughter, Horatia, at Sir William's Piccadilly home.

Lost cities

Today, the archaeological sites of Herculaneum and Pompeii, both close to Naples, are an enormous draw for tourists. They were significant for early Grand Tourists too but they acquired a new political significance when the Bourbon monarchy took charge of the Kingdom of Naples in 1734. Just as Rome's ancient architecture, obelisks and artefacts were re-used to assert the city's pedigree and legitimize papal power, the Bourbon rulers turned to their own treasures to glorify their regime and reinvent the city as 'the Florence of the South'.

Abandoned excavations at Herculaneum were re-started in 1738 when King Charles III of Spain despatched Rocco Gioacchino de Alcubierre, a surveying engineer, on a mission to supply the Spanish court with antique treasures.

Visitors to the sites were appalled by the treatment of the workers and the working methods. After a trip to Herculaneum Robert Adam observed: 'Upon the whole the subterranean town, once filled with temples, columns, palaces and other ornaments of good taste, is now exactly like a coal-mine worked by galley slaves.' Fake digs were also staged so that Grand Tourists could experience the thrill of discovery in more salubrious conditions. The Temple of Isis – discovered in 1764 and used by Mozart, who visited Naples the same year, as the setting for

This page and opposite
Wandering the streets of Herculaneum. The remains are so complete it's easy to imagine what life was like before the volcano struck.

Act I of *The Magic Flute* – was a particularly popular 'find', and two subsequent 'excavations' followed its initial discovery to satisfy visitor demand.

Archaeology, if you can call it that, began in the area in the early eighteenth century. After some initial tunnelling in 1709 (following Carlo Fontana's early explorations in the late 1500s), digging really took off with de Alcubierre. His job was to search for carved architectural marble and statuary that could be used for the king's new palace right next door to Herculaneum. The volcanic rock here is hard. I can testify to that having visited the current archaeological dig in Herculaneum, which is painstaking and slow. (Moreover, the dampness in the rock leaves exposed masonry and frescoes vulnerable to 'salting' or efflorescence, the build up of furry deposits on newly dug archaeology, as water-borne salts migrate to freshly-exposed surfaces.)

Alcubierre's tunnelling and random raiding of what he found is crude by modern standards and for that matter appeared crude then. Horace Walpole, Winckelmann and Goethe, among many others, grumbled at the careless and unscholarly approach and at the petty security measures (they were forbidden from drawing or taking notes when visiting the sites). It is partly their call for more systematic approaches that led to the birth of scientific archaeology.

Digging in Pompeii, meanwhile, got going in 1748. The archaeology there was easier: the ground was softer, consisting mainly of ash, not petrified mud and volcanic rock as at Herculaneum. It was also drier and therefore easier to conserve works that were discovered. So not surprisingly, focus shifted from Herculaneum to Pompeii. Herculaneum has remained the (unwarranted) dowdier sister of the two ever since.

The Eruption of Vesuvius by Abraham Pether 1756–1812. The ruin of Pompeii has always been attributed to Vesuvius but vulcanologist William Hamilton was the first to argue that its neighbour, Monte Somma, was in fact to blame.

Below The mountain looms over the ruins of the forum.

But the eighteenth-century excitement of Herculaneum and Pompeii started a revolution in interior design. Architects and Grand Tourists became the agents for a process by which the trappings of the upper-class Roman lifestyle were lifted from the lava and revived in the British home.

Herculanean statuary, door handles and candelabra were exactly copied. Sir John Soane popularized 'Pompeii Red', the colour of a piece of stucco found on site, in his house at Lincoln's Inn Fields. Classical enthusiasts including Robert Adam and Piranesi (who was a friend and illustrated Adam's own catalogue) reproduced motifs from architecture, wall-paintings and stucco work in catalogues and pattern books. Josiah Wedgewood chanced upon some illustrations of Sir William Hamilton's vases and never looked back, replicating their 'elegant simplicity' in homeware for a British mass market. British neoclassicism combined archaeology with manufacturing to produce, effectively, branded ranges of household goods that could be deemed authentically ancient in design and inspiration. Anyone could buy a door handle and fancifully imagine that it might have been touched by a Roman Senator.

The discovery of the Temple of Isis in 1764. The event was such a hit with Grand Tourists that two subsequent 'excavations' were staged to allow visitors to 'experience' the thrill of the discovery themselves.

Eighteenth-century excavators were horrified to discover erotic frescos, mosaics, statuary and phallic carvings in the ruins of Pompeii.

Ancient erotica and phallic cults

It has to be said, however, that inspiration from unearthed archaeological household items was edited. Roman life, it turned out, was more open, more licentious and more pagan than some eighteenth-century delicate sensibilities could cope with. Unearthed brothels in Pompeii showed depictions of bestiality, oral sex and hermaphrodites – not to mention elegant poetic graffiti which, variously, roughly translated as 'Celadus the Thracier makes the girls moan' and 'Myrtis, you do great blow jobs'.

And then, distinct from the depictions of sexual couplings, there was the vigorous adoption of priapic objects into everyday life. Here, it is important to draw some clear lines between how sexual organs were depicted in Ancient Rome. The pornographic images described above were the ones to which, frankly, we most easily relate nowadays. Erotic images to turn you on, usually involving two or more individuals.

Then there was the depiction of genitalia on statuary – small limp penises and inconsequential breasts – designed deliberately to not distract the viewer and instead subjugate desire and arousal to appreciation of ideal form, the perfect abstract human body in the image of the gods. Think of those improving statues in the British Museum again.

The third category of prick is one that befuddled the eighteenth-century mind. Almost every house in Pompeii had a lamp in the form of a giant phallus, sometimes attached to a laughingly disproportionate figure of a dwarf, hunchback, African or Oriental (all of which were considered odd, charmed or magical). Pompeiian shops had erect brick pricks modelled into their façades; one I saw was portrayed in bas-relief stucco in a miniature pavilion ready to spurt, as though it were a heavy artillery gun ready to rotate and direct its load against enemy insurgents.

Which is exactly the purpose of the phalli. To protect against evil spirits, see off curses, witches' spells, ill winds and general bad vibes. Just as in modern day Naples you can buy a string of plastic red 'chilli peppers' (hot and potent!) to bring good luck (or rather chase evil away) so a pink painted penis at the ready – or even better, a lit bronze lamp phallus – would carry all the potency and renewing regenerative power of nature that sexual imagery suggested.

Eighteenth-century excavators discovered frescoes, mosaics, statuary and a bewildering array of phallic objects, all of them, effectively, devoted to Priapus, the god of fertility and protector of gardens, who was cursed – or blessed, depending on your point of view – with an outlandishly outsize phallus.

The most enlightened contemporary scholars set about serious study of these finds, concluding that the phallic fixation should be understood as votive rather than erotic. In 1786, the Dilettante Society, which had evolved from a forum for Englishmen to relive their experiences of the Grand Tour into a formidable champion of classical antiquity and arts, published *An Account of the Remains of the Worship of Priapus,* an illustrated treatise showing votive art from the Naples area. This daring work by Richard Payne Knight argued that all art is grounded in religion, and all religion in sexuality—or 'the worship of the generative powers'.

Of course, the popular press responded with scathing attacks on collectors of antiquities in general and the Dilettanti in particular, fuelled by the Society's unabashed enthusiasm for erotic curiosities and its hedonistic bent. Payne Knight's personal history gives some indication of what may have gone on behind the closed doors of connoisseur expatriates. In a youthful poem he expresses regret for having wasted time on 'gentleman jockeys' and admits that 'ungovern'd passions led my soul astray'.

And the outcome of the controversy? Taking no chances, the authorities despatched the offending artefacts that Payne Knight had so eloquently recorded and had engraved, to a locked room in Naples' Royal Museum, with entry confined to those deemed to be of upstanding character and integrity. But the censorship proved counterproductive. Curiosity had been aroused and the idea circulated that Pompeii was a dissolute and libertine place – a myth which persists to this day.

Below Modern-day academics such as Professor Antonio Varone who has been deciphering Pompeii and its erotic art for the past 25 years, are convinced that the phallic fixation should be understood as votive rather than erotic.

The Greek connection

The history of Etruscan rule in Southern Italy and the importance of the area to Roman aristocracy suggested to early excavators that they were unearthing cultural clues to those two civilizations. But experts such as Hamilton and Winckelmann were quick to identify the influence of Ancient Greece in the quality of the vases, in writing and decoration, and in mythological stories depicted on artefacts and walls.

The eighteenth-century Grand Tourist may have witnessed the dawn of the great age of archaeology; he may have marvelled at classical architecture and statues; he may even have unearthed ancient artefacts himself. But discoveries like Herculaneum and Pompeii posed more questions than they answered. They pointed to another culture altogether – one which was tantalizingly out of reach. Until the mid-eighteenth century almost nobody went to Greece. It was part of the Ottoman Empire and not an easy or safe place for the Western traveller.

But as Naples and Italy fell to Britain's arch-enemy Napoleon, a few intrepid travellers, including members of the Dilettante Society, opened up routes to Greece and explored it for the first time. Known as the Levant Lunatics, they went in search of the ultimate classical civilization – a culture which they believed to be more magnificent, more cultivated, more pure than anything they had seen before.

Archaeologists attribute the birth of the ancient city of Paestum, fifty miles to the south of Naples, to seventh century BC Greek colonists. Before Greece itself could be visited, buildings such as the Temple of Hera were all the Grand Tourist could know of Ancient Greece.

From Piraeus to **Athens,** the Acropolis and trying out a camera obscura

A liberal attitude under Turkish rule promised sensual pleasure, and the plethora of ruins a chance to view Greek architecture as the legacy of an idealized past.

Athens in the eighteenth century was an outpost of Constantinople and something of a gateway to the East: a place of coffee houses, Turkish baths, mosques and bazaars. Administered by the Sultanic Harem, the city was famous for its liberal attitudes, holding the promise of sexual experiences that Brits could only dream about back home. Of course reality didn't always live up to its sensuous promise. After visiting one of Athens' many Turkish baths, Lady Elizabeth Craven harrumphed 'I think I never saw so many fat women together.'

Byron, who was eventually to inhabit 'the clime of the East' both intellectually and emotionally popularized the notion of travel as a personal odyssey, adding fuel to the Grand Tourist's belief that 'going East' wasn't simply a voyage of cultural discovery but an opportunity to immerse themselves in a more sensual attitude to life – a welcome respite from the restricted mores of English society.

Going native, visitors donned local costume – being Turkish at that time. In a letter written in 1795 the traveller and classical scholar John Bacon Sawrey Morritt wrote: 'I am at this moment *à la Turque* and have been for some weeks. I shall alarm you by telling you that your shawl makes a magnificent turban.... a fine ermine pelisse with my other long robes makes a very fine Turk of me, and I strut about the streets of Athens with great effect.'

Then, as now, Grand Tourists enjoyed the colour and local costumes. Guards at the presidential palace keep the tradition alive.

But Greek customs under Turkish rule were also in evidence. During and after the Greek War of Independence, Greek dance became synonymous with national identity, with each island and community developing its own forms, matched by local styles of dress. As you might expect, some Grand Tourists disdained the traditional Greek dance, inaccurately called the Romaika. Byron moaned about 'the dull round-about of the Greeks' while Turner dismissed it as 'the stupidest dance ever invented'. But others joined in, with gusto, relishing the opportunity to shed their English reserve.

And there was a more scholarly agenda. Arbiters of European taste had started to view Greek architecture as the symbol of democracy, a legacy of an idealized past. No matter that Ancient Greece had enjoyed a relatively brief tenure of democracy, operating for much of its existence as a republic; in 1751–54 the Dilettante Society financed two British architects, James Stuart and Nicholas Revett, to measure and illustrate the ancient ruins of Greece. Braving pirates, kidnapping, and a hostile Ottoman Empire at the height of its powers, the young Stuart and Revett acquired enough material to fill four large volumes, published as *The Antiquities of Athens* (1762). Scholarly, accurate and precise, it became *the* sourcebook for Ancient Greek architecture and encouraged countless British architects to travel to Greece and study the ruins for themselves. You can now buy a newly published facsimile from Princeton University Press.

Bazaars, minarets and mosques:
a legacy of the Ottoman rule of
the Grand Tour days.

Stuart and Revett did not travel unprepared. They went armed with extensive notes, not least from Pausanias' *Guide to Ancient Greece*, a helpful guide to the classical sites and local customs, history, religion and art. Admittedly it had been written in the second century AD, a legacy of perhaps the original Grand Tour generation. On completing their formal education, it seems that young Roman men often took a Mediterranean Grand Tour to sites such as Delphi, the Parthenon, Olympia and the pyramids of Giza: a Grand Tour which would have informed the art and architecture of Ancient Rome.

My guide Gregory Valliianatos shows me the sights of Athens – still a huge outdoor archeological museum. The elegant Tower of the Winds (opposite) was especially influential in Britain following its depiction in Stuart and Revett's *Antiquities of Athens*.

Opposite, bottom left, is a version of the Tower of the Winds James Stuart created for Shugborough in Staffordshire. Another was built at Mountstewart in Co. Down.

The Acropolis still dominates
the twenty-first century city.

The Acropolis

Then, as now, the Acropolis was Athens' star attraction. Built by the Ancient
Athenians as a symbol of the power of their city state, it held a particular appeal
for eighteenth-century Grand Tourists. In the 1700s, there were calls for political
change in Britain – a desire for a more equitable society which would replace
the excesses of an old elite with sobriety and restraint. Though Ancient Greek
democracy was neither enduring nor particularly democratic, its architecture was
regarded as being free from ecclesiastic and aristocratic associations, and hence a
suitable expression of these new democratic ideals. But visiting the Acropolis was
not an easy matter. Used as a Turkish fortress and garrison town with a mosque in
the middle of the Parthenon (and, variously, a church), it was strictly off limits to
foreigners. It had also been partially destroyed when the munitions arsenal within
it blew up during the siege by the Venetians in 1687. Grand Tourists like Stuart
and Revett had to resort to desperate measures to get there, bribing officials or

The Erechtheion — one of the Temples on the Acropolis once used as a harem by the Turkish Governor of Athens. In the foreground James Stuart is sketching. (Below left) Stuart is seen with his companions Nicholas Revett and James Dawkins, visiting the Monument of Philopappos.

Bottom left Buildings encroaching the Parthenon during the period of Turkish rule. Engraving from a sketch by James Stuart

clambering on rooftops. This was hazardous because they risked being shot at by Turkish soldiers, who would assume that the object of the exercise was to spy on women in the courtyards below. So the dangers were real enough: coming to eighteenth-century Greece was akin to visiting Afghanistan or Iraq today.

But their tenacity was rewarded. Built by the Athenian leader Pericles in the mid-fifth century BC, the Acropolis was the greatest cultural centre of its time. Its crowning jewel, the Parthenon, was the most sacred space in the city and was, according to eighteenth-century myth, the 'perfect building' – architecture's holy grail. Stuart and Revett were both awed by it, spending their time making accurate and detailed records of the buildings, ruins and even the Turkish garrison walls. Their fastidious obsession has been handed down from each generation of architectural students and visitors. After unification, the Acropolis took on a new sacred purpose: as the symbol of a new free Greece; the democracy or republic or whatever you wanted, reborn. Even in the twentieth century that reputation remained unassailable. Le Corbusier, in his seminal modernist tract *Vers Une Architecture* begins with the Parthenon. Dorothy Parker declared it 'Just my colour, beige'.

One valuable aid to recording at least a quick impression of the sites was a camera obscura. A precursor to the modern photographic camera, this device reflected an inverted image of the outside world onto a small glass screen through a lens, establishing a composition and perspective which the artist could then trace. I used one to make a five-minute sketch of the Parthenon on some tracing paper in the sweltering 35° heat of a July afternoon. The result was as small and as blurred as the image seemed in the box, but I'm sure that with some practice and tweaking I could have started to produce some spirited renditions that at the very least I could have sold at the gate. Provided I dressed myself up 'à la Turque'. Or maybe not. The Turkish population are not exactly fully integrated in modern Greece. Athens doesn't have a single, open, purpose-built mosque in operation these days, despite several venerable mosques sitting empty on several ancient and important sites. The public view, when I asked, is that they should be perhaps pulled down. Meanwhile, there are tens of thousands of practising Moslems in the area who quietly worship in converted factory basements and each others' houses.

But back to the Polaroid camera of its time. Eighteenth-century portable models of the camera obscura were available, and used extensively by Grand Tourists and artists. Canaletto was known to have used one, as was Joshua Reynolds, who owned a camera obscura disguised as a book – a sensible precaution given that

By the eighteenth century, portable models of the camera obscura were available to help tourists and artists establish perspectives and composition. Using one of these devices I made my own accurate – but reverse – sketch of the Parthenon.

Although the marble of Athens' ancient monuments is eroded in places, the crispness and precision of the original carving is still very much in evidence.

London.

The Royal Exchange, Manchester.

British M...

Are you collecti...

Prior Park and the Palladian Bridge, Bath.

the contraption tended to provoke hysteria from locals, who screamed at the idea of their own bodies being spirited into a box. Turkish officials viewed the camera obscura as a tool for stealing the Parthenon with the aid of the devil's magic, and prohibited its use, though a bribe would generally persuade them to change their minds.

Drawing aids, the archaeological survey work of Stuart and Revett and the subsequent enthusiastic discoveries by countless interested amateurs, led to something of a Greek building boom in Britain. The Greek Revival in Britain really took off in the first few decades of the nineteenth century, just as the industrial revolution was taking hold and emerging cities like Liverpool and Birmingham were looking for an appropriate architecture to express their no-nonsense civic values, their pride in new-found local democratic ideas and their accessibility. The manly columns of the Parthenon were chunky, devoid of spurious, mouldings and decorations and right for their job. Other more complex Greek temples provided alternative inspiration. It was right in the new age of public buildings, of institutions, art galleries, town halls and museums, to adopt this purer, sterner style over the more decorative and lighter Roman architecture that Robert Adam had popularized from the 1760s onwards. Sir Robert Smirke's British Museum (1823–1852) and Thomas Hamilton's Old Royal High School in Edinburgh (1826–1829) represented this new neoclassical Greek Doric style. The latter was even built on the south face of Calton Hill as part of Edinburgh's Acropolis.

259   LONDON. — St. Paul's Cathedral (West Front) — LL.

Inspired by classical architecture, new buildings in Britain and across Europe became tourist sights themselves, celebrated on countless postcards.

Left Edinburgh's Calton Hill with Thomas Hamilton's Royal High School of 1826–1859 in the Greek Doric style. The National Monument to commemorate the fallen in the Napoleonic Wars sits squarely above it. Also started in 1826 it was intended to be a replica of the Parthenon, but money ran out three years later.

As well as removing the marbles from the Parthenon, Lord Elgin took one of the caryatids from the Erectheion to adorn his Scottish mansion.

The Erectheion, an ancient Greek temple on the north side of the Acropolis built between 421 and 407 BC and used as a harem by the Turkish Governor of Athens, was also the source of much inspiration and found a contemporary British counterpart in St Pancras New Church in London (1819–22), designed by the father-and-son team William and Henry Inwood, who had both spent time in Greece. Giant (and, it has to be said, sterner) copies of the caryatids, the elegant female figures who guarded the Erectheion's porch, support protruding vestries on the north and south sides of the church. They're still there over the road from Euston station. These caryatids, representations of young girls paraded before the single men of ancient Athens, have something of a story.

They were copied, we know, for the Roman Emperor Hadrian, who had the reproductions installed in his villa at Tivoli. The copies of course have been ransacked and damaged but twentieth-century second copies exist and I was lucky enough on my trip to Tivoli to be able to take a mould of a tiny detail of

The caryatids were copied by the father-and-son architectural team of William and Henry Inwood for the vestries of their St Pancras New Church in London.

Far right A rash of caryatids sprang up throughout Britain. Some have been captured on a postcard of Montpellier Walk, Cheltenham.

The New Acropolis Museum, designed by Swiss architect
Bernard Tschumi, opened in 2009, its sweeping porch
pointing squarely at the Acropolis. It includes an empty
room awaiting the Elgin marbles' eventual return.

one of the caryatids, a sandaled foot. My purpose was really just to demonstrate to the camera how an eighteenth-century copyist might take a mould to later form a plaster cast of an ancient statue. Meanwhile, I should add, one of the original caryatids from the Acropolis did find its way to Britain, removed by Lord Elgin, British Ambassador to the Ottoman Empire from 1799–1803, to decorate his Scottish mansion. According to Athenian legend, the five remaining caryatids could be heard wailing for their lost sister, something that didn't prevent Elgin from later attempting to remove a second caryatid, and having it sawn into pieces when technical difficulties arose. The originals have now been transferred to safety in the New Acropolis Museum – a building by Swiss architect Bernard Tschumi that opened in 2009. The caryatids in the Erectheion are now themselves copies of the originals. Both originals and copies are severely eroded, to the point where they don't have sandalled feet any more but just blobs. Meanwhile, I have been able to cast in plaster feet that are copies of copies of first-century AD copies *but* they are at least of a recognizable foot, which means I have a missing chunk of one of the caryatids, a coup which my eleven-year-old son describes as boring – but I consider quite cool.

Thomas Bruce, seventh Earl of Elgin: hero or vandal? The 'Elgin Marbles' saga, whereby Elgin 'liberated' antique treasures from the Parthenon, divided opinion in British society. After a heated debate in parliament they ended up on display in the British Museum.

But crimes against caryatids were the least of Lord Elgin's misdemeanours. His most audacious act, the 'liberation' of the Elgin marbles, was the controversy of the Grand Tour. Having persuaded the Sultan of Constantinople to grant him access to the Acropolis for £5 a day – about £500 today – Elgin oversaw the removal of countless Antique treasures, including around half of the surviving sculptures in the Parthenon. And he destroyed parts of the building in the process. He claimed to have had a formal permit but it was never produced and he was only able to offer a copy of an Italian translation of the original. Like my foot.

So following a public debate in parliament over the probity of Elgin's methods, the 'Elgin Marbles' were purchased by the British government in 1816 and placed on display in the British Museum. Elgin countered accusations of vandalism by claiming to have an official mandate. Since his agreement with the sultan was conveniently destroyed, the veracity of his claim could never be determined. In any case, there were bigger issues at play than contractual small print. Elgin claimed the moral high ground, arguing that his actions were designed to preserve the ruins from mismanagement by the Turks and to 'improve British taste'. Patriotism overcame many misgivings: the Scottish author John Galt wrote 'I was greatly vexed and disappointed by the dilapidation of the temple of Minerva; but I am consoled by the reflection that the spoils are destined to ornament our own land, and that, if they had not been taken possession of by Lord Elgin, they would probably have been carried away by the French'. The gallery in the British Museum where the marbles now rest illustrates the same point, showing damage wrought to remaining marble panels on the Parthenon after Elgin had left.

Others, including Lord Byron who denounced Elgin as a 'vandal', viewed his actions as symptomatic of the systematic plundering which has plagued the Parthenon since ancient times. The legality – and moral probity – of Elgin's actions remains in dispute. The New Acropolis Museum contains an empty room awaiting their eventual return. And the Greek government, mindful of the incredible patriotic importance of the Acropolis, the extent of the long frieze taken, the number of important figures from the pediments in the UK and (most importantly for other worried museums around the world guarding their own plunder of one kind or another) the sensitivities and complexities of 'repatriating' works of art, have offered Britain a wide choice of replacement objects from other Greek museums.

The marbles that are now on display in the British Museum and in Athens were from the pediments of the Parthenon.

Travel in Greece was uncomfortable and sometimes dangerous. Tourists would visit the more remote sites on horseback and set up makeshift campsites on the way.

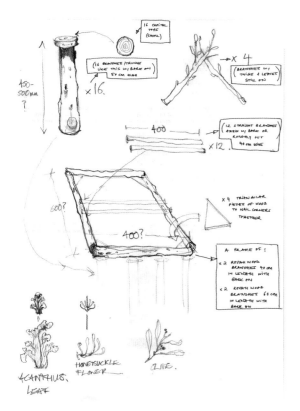

Aegina

Between 1803 and 1815, the Napoleonic Wars rendered Italy largely off limits to British travellers. So not surprisingly, Greece became inundated with Grand Tourists – often self-styled as archaeologists and treasure hunters – in search of new territories to explore. But travelling in Greece remained something of a challenge. Tourists were prey to pirates, plague and Turks – Lady Elizabeth Craven travelled with two 'most excellent pistols' stuffed into her girdle – or simple discomfort. Benjamin Disraeli wrote to his father in 1830: 'I can give you no idea of the severe hardship and privation of the present Grecian travel. Happy are we to get a shed for nightly shelter, and never have been fortunate enough to find one not swarming with vermin. My sufferings in this way are great'.

Horse trains were employed for journeys into the wilderness, with horses laden down with makeshift campsites, mosquito nets and pots and pans. The ride was far from comfortable: Greek saddles were not the saddles we know today, but thin bars of wood bound together with leather straps and covered in sticking out nails. But Tourists were not to be deterred. Travelling in the 'outback' fired the imagination. Acutely aware that they were following in the footsteps not only of Ancient Greek architects but also their poets (Homer) and classical heroes, tourists were sustained by the belief that the ruins of Ancient Greece, being older than Roman architecture, held those hidden truths about the origins not just of architecture but of civilization itself.

These beliefs were additionally fuelled by theories, devised in France by a monk called Laugier in the early eighteenth century, and promoted by such luminaries as Lord Burlington – that all Greek temple architecture had grown from simple wooden structures contrived from trunks and branches, and decorated with leaves and flowers. These devices, it was suggested, had eventually over centuries been carved into the timber and the entire tradition carried over into stone. Greece is cursed with few forests and blessed with much good marble so it's easy to give these theories credence. And indeed a lot of patterned detailing on classical temples suggests very functional, timber components of building: nails, brackets, joist ends and spreader plates for supporting beams.

Conveniently, no timber temples survive to test this theory, but there are a number of conclusions that it is safe to draw about Greek architecture. The early style, from around 500 BC, of the Parthenon is closer to Egyptian temple design than to wooden shacks. There are many stylistic influences from across the Mediterranean, such as the broad, shallow and undecorated capitals that crown the columns and act as those 'spreader plates' to take the load of the stone blocks or beams above.

Marc-Antoine Laugier transformed architectural practice with his *Essai sur l'Architecture* in which he argued that the primitive hut was the origin of western architecture. My sketch (opposite) shows the way in which plants, flowers and wood can create the structure and ornament of a primitive temple.

Above An eighteenth-century engraving of a primitive hut.

Then, as Greece developed and labour and talent became more available, the decoration evolved with more and more detail from nature being copied into the stone. Daisies, acanthus leaves, ropes, reeds, leaves and berries were lovingly carved into later stonework, alongside bas-relief and fully modelled statuary.

And this is perhaps the moment to bust another myth about classical architecture. The heroes of this book, Palladio, Jones, Adam and many others spent their architectural lives trying to sort classical buildings out into neat styles. The sequence that most of them settled on ran: Tuscan, Doric, Ionic, Corinthian, Composite, a series of styles that was supposedly chronological and increasingly more developed. Frankly, it was based on Roman architecture more than anything else and it was anything but tidy. It is impossible to put each of these orders in any kind of order. They developed and mutated and influenced each other. When I wandered around the Agora in Athens, admiring the much-copied Tower of the Four Winds, I came across a row of 'Corinthian' capitals (see page 153) that had been dug up. They were obviously from different buildings because the carved leaves took every form imaginable. Each capital was different in style, complexity, size and verisimilitude. There was no order to put them in.

The Temple of Aphaia

For English architects, Greek travel also offered a commercial incentive. With classical designs much in demand at home, first-hand knowledge of Greek architecture offered a valuable competitive edge. One such architect, Charles Robert Cockerell (1788–1863) who arrived in Greece in 1810 in his early twenties, and travelled to the island of Aegina in 1811. According to Greek mythology, the island had been inhabited since Zeus enjoyed a romantic liaison with the maiden Aegina. Zeus populated the island with Myrmidons – men created from ants – so that Aecaus, his son by Aegina, would have subjects in his kingdom. The island was also the birthplace of Achilles and Ajax, the great Classical heroes of the Trojan War. So the place was crawling with history as well as ants.

The temple of Aphaia on the island of Aegina: the English architect C.R. Cockerell astonished – and horrified – his fellow Antiquarians with the discovery that the pure white marble forms were originally covered in garish paint.

To Cockerell and his companions, including Baron Haller von Hallerstein, architect to the King of Bavaria, the island was a treasure trove not just of myth but of sculpture and carving. As soon as they arrived they set about the excavation of the island's temple dating from around 510–490 BC, later identified as the Temple of Aphaia, goddess of the whole earth and protector of sailors and hunters. Within three weeks of their arrival on Aegina, they had unearthed all of the temple's ancient marbles, including its ornamental pediment which they discovered, untouched, three feet below ground within days of beginning their dig. Imagine a twenty-two-year-old architecture student from Cardiff or Nottingham digging up an entire temple on his gap year nowadays.

And there was more to astonish. From his study of the ruins, Cockerell concluded that the temple's ornamental features were originally covered in garish paint, a shocking discovery which rocked the antiquarian world of that time. This young adventurer was not only digging up ruins with a view to making a fortune and advancing his career, but he was also all of a sudden contributing to the discipline of art history. Winckelmann, who, despite never actually visiting Greece, was revered as a leading authority on its Ancient architecture, had always maintained that Ancient Greek buildings were white and pure. The revelation that they were coloured, and even gaudy, constituted an affront to their dignity and timelessness. Purity withstands the test of time; paint falls off and fades. The notion of these temples as sacred representations of some ancient noble truth was beginning to crumble.

The controversy fuelled a frenzy of interest. International studies concluded that Greek design was more sensual than had previously been thought. We now know that temples were richly adorned, not just with paint but with glass, jewels, flags and devotional objects. When the Danish Hansen family of architects came to redesign the academy, university and library buildings in the newly asserted Greek capital after the War of Independence, their buildings were painted, muralled and gilded. They still today suggest a style of architecture that is jollier and more celebratory than the naked Parthenon suggests.

Meanwhile, Cockerell's party evidently had no qualms about selling their spoils; in his journal, *Travels in Southern Europe and the Levant, 1810–17* he wrote: 'We conduct all our affairs with respect to them in the utmost secrecy, for fear The Turk should either reclaim them or put difficulties in the way of our exporting them'. In the event, the British Museum was undecided as to whether classical archaeology was a legitimate investment and the treasures were sold, on Baron Haller von Hallerstein's advice, to the Crown Prince Ludwig of Bavaria. They are currently on display in Munich's Glyptothek Museum.

Greek Revival

Set in verdant pinewoods with commanding views of the sea, the Temple of Aphaia exemplified the Greek approach to the site. Where Roman architecture was more urban, its external expression often amounting to little more than a single façade, the Greeks conceived their temples as three-dimensional objects in the landscape. Imposing from every angle, they were placed on mountain tops, between symmetrical hills, in valleys and on mounds, depending on which god or godesses that they represented. But it was their three-dimensionality and their solidity that made them the perfect role model for British cultural buildings designed to convey civic pride, cultural objects in their own right rather than buildings which could be absorbed into a street façade.

Buildings such as Birmingham Town Hall, designed by the architects Joseph Hansom (Hansom cab fame) and Edward Welch, as a home for the Birmingham Triennial Music Festival (1832–1834), owe their stately gravitas to monuments such as the Temple of Aphaia – which was built for a nymph. There's nothing much nymphly about the Methodism of the industrial north or the earnestness of patrician city fathers bent on cultural improvement.

Cockerell, who coined the term 'Greek Revival' himself, went on to design several significant civic buildings in Britain including the Ashmolean Museum in Oxford, the Fitzwilliam Museum in Cambridge and St George's Hall in Liverpool. The British Museum, repository for all things Greek in Britain is a scholarly essay in stone by Robert Smirke. The Burns Monument on Calton Hill in Edinburgh by Thomas Hamilton is a reverential copy of the Lysicrates Monument in Athens, also reproduced at Shugborough Hall in Staffordshire. British Greek Revival buildings weren't so much inspired by Greek originals as imaginative copies of them. Architects had fallen in love with the new discipline of archaeology and embodied its respect for buildings as historical documents in their own work.

The thing is, Greek temples were built for worship on islands drenched by brilliant sunlight. Greek Revival buildings hid their windows and doorways behind severe colonnades and porticos. The High School in Edinburgh by Hamilton, built in 1825, looks like a mausoleum. It is now blackened on the outside and has always been pretty gloomy on the inside. An architecture designed to create shade from the heat and glare isn't quite so effective at introducing light to the desks and benches of a Scottish school. It soon became obvious that the 'perfect' Greek architecture being imported was less than adequate under the dim grey skies of Britain – where not even the crisp carving of a capital could be properly admired without the sharp warm rays of a boiling Levantine sun.

A camp of Philhellenes – foreign supporters of the Greek cause in its battle for independence from Turkey. Of the 940 known Philhellenes, about a third were German, the others were French, Italian, British and American.

The poets Lord Byron (left) and Percy Bysshe Shelley were two high-profile British visitors who threw in their lot with the Greek War of Independence.

Fighting for freedom

Independence for Greece was an inevitable discussion point for the British in the Levant. Over time, as more Grand Tourists were seduced by the lure of Ancient Greece, the attitude towards the Turkish occupation changed. Convinced that modern Greeks were the lineal descendants of ancient Greeks and that Turks were barbarians, Grand Tourists encouraged the local Greek population to revolt against their Ottoman 'enslavers' in the great Greek War of Independence which raged from 1821 until 1829. Proxy patriotism was rife, with many Grand Tourists identifying with the Greeks and playing a direct role in the crusade. The introduction to *Hellas*, written by Shelley and published to raise funds for the war, asserted: 'We are all Greeks…our laws, our literature, our religion, our arts have their roots in ancient Greece.' Shelley died in 1822 in a shipwreck off the coast of Italy on the way to Greece. Byron, who spent £4,000 of his own money on refitting the Greek fleet, died from fever on the ruins at Messolonghi in 1824, becoming an instant martyr to the cause and prompting countless other Brits to join the fight. As I discovered, Byron is still revered as a national hero in Greece. Thus a new breed of Romantic Traveller emerged. The picturesque voyeuristic approach to travel was *démodé*. Danger and discomfort became a badge of honour. Grand Tourists sought a 'real' experience fighting and, if necessary, dying for the cause. The ultimate adventure holiday was born.

Descending by harness into the caves of **Antiparos** in the Cyclades

A natural, geological wonder, listed in the travel itineraries of the more adventurous Grand Tourists, the experience of which was sure to inspire the requisite awe and terror.

As adventure – or, more accurately, misadventure – became the very point of travel, a hardier kind of tourist emerged braving pirates, rough seas and disease to seek out far-flung destinations which were particularly difficult to visit. Inspired by Byron and the 'Levant Lunatics', they tracked down obscure relics of antiquity on rocky precipices, or in dramatic valleys They were searching for inspiration mixed with awe and terror. Antiquity and the Sublime.

Sublime as defined by Burke is a curious word. In its true (and late eighteenth-century) sense it summarized the sensation of being overawed by the terrifying power and scale of nature, of its cliffs, caves, mountains, seas and storms. A modern day gap-year student might go off in search of 'thrills' instead, bungy-jumping over crocodile-infested waters. Then, the settings of Greek temples and shrines were drama enough. Or rather, not quite enough. In the quest for the Sublime the more Romantic travellers began to view man-made art and architecture as less important than the landscapes themselves. The mountains, once viewed as perilous terrain to be avoided at any cost, became increasingly enticing, valued both for their intrinsic beauty and their geological gravitas. If ancient architecture offered insights into the birth of civilization, the mountains spoke of the formation of earth itself. Ancient history was outclassed by 'deep time'.

And so with renewed respect for nature, travellers learnt to appreciate a different kind of aesthetic – not just the awe-inspiring Sublime epitomized by Mount Vesuvius, but more capricious, fantastical forms of nature in all her glory. The cave on Antiparos in the Cyclades Islands in the middle of the Aegean Sea was one of many natural wonders which made their way onto seventeenth and eighteenth travel itineraries. Described in an 1845 guidebook to Greece as 'the greatest natural curiosity of its kind in the known world', it was a truly astonishing site. The oldest stalagmite in Europe, thought to be 45 million years old, marked the entrance to a cave which burrowed down into the rock for a 100 metres or so, leading to an underworld fairyland of rock formations and stalactites. I descended on ropes when I was there, ignoring the modern steps in an attempt to replicate the experience of a Grand Tourist 200 years ago. I abseiled cliffs, crawled through bat-infested tunnels ankle deep in their detritus and cack, and waded down scree walls. It was at times deeply unpleasant and in the dim light not a little terrifying, especially when slipping over wet rock. But there was an immense privilege in descending backwards on a rope, walking down a face of stalactite drips that looked as though the walls were made of dripping toffee. For all the world, the cave looked like a natural Perpendicular Gothic cathedral, as though the master mason of King's College Chapel had found direct inspiration for his fan vaulting here. All of a sudden I twigged how a visitor in the early 1800s would have made the direct link between this natural beauty on an enormous scale and the medieval cathedrals of Europe. Its Gothic charm was rendered all the more mystical by the flickering firelight. Flaming torches were the only illumination in its perilous pitch-black depths.

A wonder of the age, the cave had, in fact, been famous for over two millenia. The earliest visitor was said to have been Archilochos (728–650 BC), a poet from Paros, while Macedonian generals sought refuge in the cave after conspiring against Alexander the Great. It may have been a natural wonder, but to Grand Tourists it was an extension of Antiquity, and there was uproar when the Russian fleet removed some of its stalactites during the Russian occupation of 1770–1774. The fruits of this 'sacrilege against Antiquity' are now on display in the Hermitage Museum in St Petersburg.

But the Russians were not the first bounty-hunters to raid the cave. In 1673 the French Ambassador to Constantinople, Marquis de Nouadel, paid the cave a Christmas visit in the hope of unearthing archaeological finds. The cave's extraordinary beauty prompted the marquis to perform a spontaneous Mass atop a stalagmite that to me looked just like a miniature altar, placed before a giant carved reredos screen.

Like so many Grand Tourists before me I viewed these dramatic caves by the light of a flaming torch and clinging to a rope.

No wonder he felt moved to claim the depths of this place for God. So moved, in fact, that he left a Latin inscription that is still there on the stalagmite/altar translated as 'Here Christ himself celebrated Midnight Mass on Christmas 1673.'

The graffiti on the walls points to other illustrious visitors. King Otto, the first king of Greece, carved his name when he visited with his wife in 1840, while Byron and countless other British visitors added their names, in a desire to mark the achievement of just making it there in the first place. Because it *was* quite an achievement. After reaching the island by caïque and riding a donkey up the hill, visitors would be lowered into the cave by rope before climbing down rickety ladders and sliding down rocks, often cutting themselves in the process and invariably tearing their clothes. I manged to cut my arm and lacerate a leg. And *I* wasn't wearing crinoline.

Having completed the perilous journey to the depths of the cave, visitors couldn't resist carving their names in the stone. Jean Baptiste Tillard's engraving of the interior of the grotto of Antiparos captures the awe-inspiring splendour of the sight (opposite).

Caves and crinoline

And crinoline there was. Lady Elgin declined to visit the grotto claiming that 'it would be too great an undertaking for me.' Lady Craven, however, was made of sterner stuff. Author, playwright, traveller and socialite, and one of the first female Grand Tourists, she had embarked on her long travels having separated from her husband, Lord Craven, after thirteen years of marriage. Having visited Italy, Vienna, Bulgaria, Bucharest and Warsaw she arrived in Greece in 1785. Renowned for her feistiness, as well as for her beauty, Lady Craven was egged on by the French Ambassador, the Comte de Choiseul Gouffier who implored: 'Never has a woman gone down into the grotto of Antiparos, and few men have wished to make the descent; but you, Miladi, you absolutely must go down'. She gamely rose to the challenge confessing 'had it not been that my pride rose superior to my fears, I would never have gone down'.

Sailors were sent ahead to light the cave with flaming torches in advance of Lady Craven's descent. Crawling into the hole, with a strong rope fastened to the outside, she almost choked on the smoke, and had to clamber into the cave's depths in a most unladylike manner – sometimes sitting, sometimes sliding, and, in places, climbing down the perpendicular rope-ladders which were the only way to advance. But it all paid off. A self-styled Romantic traveller, with a proclaimed preference for 'Nature rather than man-made spaces', she saw the cave as the ultimate 'temple of nature', and one of the highlights of her travels.

Over the **Alps** by sedan chair

At first a terrifying journey to be endured blindfold but
latterly an eagerly anticipated experience of the Sublime,
an extreme manifestation of the Wonders of Nature.

Antiparos represented a turning point for me on my own Grand Tour; the shift from
architecture to nature as the object of historical curiosity for Grand Tourists and the
end of my own Mediterranean adventure. My route back to Britain was to be not by
sea as I had partly come, but overland, over mountains in fact. The inevitable and
dreaded part of every Grand Tour involved crossing the Alps, via any one of a number
of high passes: the French Petit or Grand St Bernard Pass, the pass via Mont Cenis
or a variety of routes through Switzerland. Throughout the seventeenth and early
eighteenth centuries it's fair to say that tourists were as terrified of the journey. But
as the interest in landscape, the Sublime and the origins of our environment took
hold so the Alps were increasingly seen as a place for adventure and discovery in their
own right. The works of Jean-Jacques Rousseau, the Geneva-born philosopher and
Enlightenment critic, also prompted visitors to consider landscape as an inspirational
and appropriate setting for inquiry.

One of the very first expeditions to the mountains of the Alps was English. In
June 1741, eight intrepid young men, armed to the teeth and dressed, somewhat
bizarrely, as Ottomans (the Greek influence was then very strong indeed among
travellers) set out from Geneva on a three-day trek to Chamonix.

Fearing the locals, the party, led by Richard Pocock and William Windham
– the former a fearless professional traveller and priest, the latter a young student

with a penchant for amateur dramatics and hell-raising around Geneva – camped outside the village, burning fires and keeping permanent watch. But the natives turned out to be friendly. Acting as mountain guides, they led the party to a spectacular 4½ mile-long glacier, named by Windham and Pocock as the Mer de Glace – the Sea of Ice. Delighted with their discovery, the Englishmen wrote an account of their trip, which was published in 1744. It sparked a Europe-wide fascination with Chamonix, putting a new Grand Tour destination firmly on the map.

A stream of European visitors followed, prompting the creation of the Company of Mountain Guides of Chamonix (who were my guides on the glacier). The locals themselves became more focussed on the Mer de Glace and its mountain, Mont Blanc, the highest in Europe at nearly 16,500 feet. They included Horace-Bénédict de Saussure (1740–1799), a Swiss aristocrat and naturalist who in 1760 offered a prize to anyone who could reach the top of the mountain. In 1786 Jacques Balmat – a local hard man and crystal hunter, clearly used to the wild environment at altitude – and a Dr Paccard from Chamonix successfully reached the summit having camped the night on the mountain. The following year de Saussure himself

The Swiss physicist and geologist Horace Bénédict de Saussure, 1740–1799, was a pioneer of Alpine exploration. The painting below shows Saussure with his son and guides, at Grand Géant glacier, Mont Blanc, where they camped for 17 days in July 1788.

made the ascent and modern alpinism had clearly begun. Foreigners, too, were interested in this wonder of nature. Goethe had visited in 1760, inspired by the writings of Rousseau; Wordsworth turned up in 1790. A tourist industry began to blossom. Chamonix opened its first guest house in 1770 and by 1783 it was receiving around 1500 visitors each summer. In the nineteenth century it started to cater for more demanding tastes: the first luxury hotel was built in 1816.

Despite the burgeoning tourist trade, the trek to the Mer de Glace was a hazardous affair involving an arduous climb by donkey. When Mary Shelley (1797-1851) visited the glacier in 1816, while eloping with her future husband the poet Percy Bysshe Shelley, they were driven back by ferocious rain and Shelley slipped and knocked himself out. When they finally made it, Mary was overawed by what she described in her diary as 'the most desolate place in the world'. Shelley wrote his own ode to the area with the poem, 'Mont Blanc: Lines Written in the Vale of Chamouni.' In the travelogue written jointly by the two of them, *History of a Six Week's Tour* (1817), it is described in rather more poetic terms: 'a scene in truth of dizzying wonder...On all sides precipitous mountains, the abodes of unrelenting frost...they pierce the clouds like things not belonging to this earth.'

We all love mountain scenery today. But that's because artists such as Swiss painter Caspar Wolf (1735–1783) taught us to see its beauty in paintings such as *The Mountains at Lauteraar* of 1776.

My own trip to the Mer de Glace wasn't too dissimilar to the Shelleys'. Although I made the ascent in August, the weather was foul and cold. By the time we arrived at the head of the donkey track (on the rack and pinion railway these days) the weather had closed in and a thick swirling mist was wrapping itself around the station. My intention had been to use a primitive camera to take a photo in imitation of the daguerrotypes that John Ruskin proudly took as a young man on his annual pilgrimage to the Alps, but the camera fogged up more than the landscape. So that idea was jettisoned, and instead we altered our plans and headed glumly through the grey down the footpath straight to the glacier, without much hope of seeing anything. It looked like the only sublime manifestation of nature that I was going to see was fog.

Previous pages An inscribed stone commemorating Richard Pocock and William Windham's trek to Mer de Glace. The two Englishmen and their party put Chamonix and the nearby Mer de Glace on the Grand Tourist map.

Our party was nine strong: myself, director and producer, assistants, camera and sound and two local *Guides de Chamonix*, all kitted out in wet-weather gear, harnesses, rucksacks and stout mountaineering boots designed to take crampons. We passed the large rock on which Windham and Pocock's names had been brazenly carved (apparently by locals after their visit) and looked out expecting to see what they had seen, a majestic white glacier in a precipitous and towering

Two views of the Mer de Glace taken from the same spot. The glacier has dropped some 300 feet since it was first engraved in the eighteenth century leaving a grey scar. The sign (right) marks its surface level in 1820.

Overleaf Returning across the ice shelf with the exposed wall, its ladders just visible, some 300 feet high, ahead of us. Opposite above and below are two views of the ice. There is an hallucinatory ambiguity of scale and orientation on the ice. A crevasse can be a metre long and deep or a hundred times that. The picture below shows the ice cave under the Mer de Glace but bears a striking resemblance to the vertical moulin into which I descended.

mountain landscape of impossible peaks reaching vertically from us to 4,500 metres.

But there was nothing. Even when the mist cleared a little there was still nothing. Just air. I began to think the light and mist were playing tricks on us but of course the glacier is a shadow of what it was. Climate change has reduced its height over the last century or so to 300 feet below its former level. To access it we had to rope up, descend four ladders bolted into the cliff face and traverse ledges to arrive, forty minutes later, at the ice shelf. The last four metres were by rope: the latest ladder, installed ten years ago, is now already too short.

A world of ice may be majestic and glinting in the sun but in mist and fog it is an ambiguous and monochrome world, where rock faces seem to be ice walls and crevasses deceptively appear as gently formed depressions. It is impossible to figure out the scale of anything. With crampons on, we trod gingerly, spending seven hours on the ice. We slowly climbed the glacier's terrain, a surface like a giant ploughed field littered with stones and boulders until we arrived at our real destination to meet Luc, a glaciologist who was testing the depth of a moulin.

A moulin is an odd and seductive thing, a star-shaped set of crevasses that meet and melt into a hole in the surface of the glacier, a hole that can extend hundreds of metres vertically down into the ice. It is part of the plumbing of a glacier, carrying meltwater down into a place that, if you fell into it, would swallow you forever *just* as it swallows the gallons of water a second that cascade into it off the ice. It is a noisy, dangerous piece of territory, where walls of ice turn gently from white to turquoise blue to intense inky black as you stare down and down into the bowels of a glacier; Dante's ultimate frigid circle of hell.

Luc had tied himself to a rock to test how far down hell was and figured it was getting on for 500 feet. Olivier, one of our guides, rolled an enormous boulder over the sloping edge of one of the tributary crevasses and we waited for the noise of it hitting the bottom. After what seemed an age it boomed. And then four seconds later boomed again. And then again. This seemed as inhospitable a place you could find on the planet. Which is why my producer suggested I climb down it.

I enjoy abseiling because it involves letting gravity assist you gently in getting to the bottom of something – like a cliff or building – undoing your harness and walking away invigorated and ten inches taller. It looks macho and doesn't require enormous effort. The idea of abseiling into something from which you then have to climb out on toe crampons while grappling your way up an ice wall with two ice axes while getting drenched by a sub-zero waterfall is terrifying. I hated the abseil, descending fifty feet or so and then stopping. Below that was hell and below that was the boulder. My memory is of a star-shaped icy mouth disappearing into blackness beckoning me down to frozen oblivion. The noise of rushing water was intense and I could hear nothing of the shouts or instructions from my companions on the surface. I took photographs, a nervous video; I prepared myself to try to descend lower but then realized that below me was an overhang which I knew I'd have difficulty climbing if I dropped too far. So I started, inexpertly, to ice climb the wall with my axes, looking at the broken fragments kicked away by crampons as they dropped below me. The climb seemed to last for half an hour but was probably five minutes and on emerging back into the now welcoming mist and drizzle I felt huge, huge relief.

I also experienced another two extraordinary sensations: first, cold, intense cold as the adrenalin sapped away and the effects of hanging in a freezer took hold; then a calmer but powerful sense of terror, of being overwhelmed by what I had just seen. Luc shook my hand, saying: 'your first moulin has the biggest effect of all. Well done.' I couldn't reply. It dawned on me that I was experiencing, for the first time in my life, the very thing that had preoccupied Rousseau, Shelley, Goethe and Burke. I now knew what the word 'Sublime' means.

Mary Shelley was able to respond to this experience with more creativity and resonance than anybody. In her Gothic novel *Frankenstein* (1818), which she had started writing while staying with her friend Lord Byron a month before her visit, Victor Frankenstein sets off for Chamonix in search of peace and relief from his 'sullen despair'. There is an encounter with the monster on the ice, a denouement. Mary paints the monster as representative of many things: the monster that was the French Revolution and, for that matter, humanity; representative also of the ultimate inevitable consequence of man's preoccupation with science, of the Enlightenment. But I can vouch for the fact that the ice, not the monster, is the true terror, because it represents the original power of nature over all things. If I'd met the monster down there I'd have lent him an ice axe.

Where the Shelleys' saw 'things not belonging to this earth', scientists saw a legacy of something else. The Romantic period of poetry and the Sublime grew in opposition to much of what the Enlightenment's scientific method of enquiry, promoting instead the value of experience and intuition. At the same time new sciences like geology and Luc's glaciology, were revealing truths about ancient history that was much older than the Greeks. In the nineteenth century the Swiss scientist Jean Louis Rodolphe Agassiz (1807–1873), drawing on his studies of the Alpine glaciers, was the first to prove the existence of the Ice Age, while British scientists such as Scotsman Professor J.D. Forbes (1809–1868) and Irishman John

Opposite The Mer de Glace makes its way majestically and imperceptibly downhill carrying vast screes of rocks and boulders on its flanks as powerful a force of nature now, though a fraction of its size, as it appeared to the Grand Tourists.

The great Victorian critic and social commentator John Ruskin: as well as making daguerreotypes of the Alpine scenery, he captured its beauty in impressionistic sketches such as *Moonlight, Chamonix* painted in 1866.

Tyndall (1820–1893) made their own forays into the mountains, in a quest for knowledge about the forces that created the earth's lofty landscapes. 'Old-earth' was a concept propounded by Sir Charles Lyell (1797–1875). Known as the father of modern geology, Lyell visited Mer de Glace in 1818 (the same year as the publication of *Frankenstein*), recording observations and collecting fossils and rocks in a bid to support his – then radical – concept that geological and biological forces had always been at work.

That idea was to have a profound impact on the history of science. Lyell's old-earth theories greatly informed the concept of evolution developed by Charles Darwin (1809–1882), and he and Darwin became friends and professional allies. When Darwin published *On the Origin of Species* (1859), his controversial tract on evolution and natural selection, Lyell was one of the first scientists to voice his support.

I'm aware that on this last leg of my Grand Tour I haven't followed one man on a single-purposed vision or quest but a series of adventurous individuals. Design and architecture have taken a back seat as nature and poetry have taken over. New sciences have confounded old dogmas, and art and sculpture have been relegated. So where do all these strands lead? Where do glaciology, the Sublime, buildings and art all meet? The answer is in one man. John Ruskin.

Ruskin (1819–1900) was an extraordinary man, a gifted prodigy. The son of a wealthy sherry importer, his interest in the outside world began when his father gave him a set of geological crystals as a boy. By the time he was 21 he was a Fellow of the Geological Society. But when aged only 17, he had had a paper published on comparisons between the vernacular architectural styles of Northern Europe (focussing especially on the distinctions between English and Alpine farmhouses), *The Poetry of Architecture*. He was an avid and talented artist, a lover of nature and a huge fan of J.W.M. Turner the artist (1775–1851), who was some four decades older. Ruskin used his influence to promote Turner, to persuade his father to support Turner and himself during his lifetime, and was able to use his inherited fortune to acquire over 300 works by this one artist.

In championing Turner – at a time when his work was sneered at – Ruskin found his first great vocation. He was able to take the visual ideas of a man who had famously tied himself to a ship's mast to experience the full sublime terror of a sea storm, and connect them through his own passions, to the new emerging sciences of optics, geology and meteorology. He was so adoring of the old artist that as an impressionable adolescent he had drawn a view of an Alpine pass in direct imitation of Turner's same view. Ruskin enjoyed a

The artist J.M.W. Turner revelled in the extreme weather conditions of the Alps, as in the painting above of travellers caught in a snowdrift on Mount Tarrar. He was particularly drawn to St Gotthard's Pass, with its plunging waterfalls and precipices. The view below shows Devil's Bridge and St Gotthard's Pass and on the opposite page the view from the bridge itself.

privileged upbringing, travelling every year with his parents and later in life visiting the Alps almost annually.

Turner's experience of Alpine landscapes was more limited. But travelling through the Alps in 1802, when the Treaty of Amiens temporarily halted hostilities between England and France, he had been mesmerized by the scenery, particularly in the St Gotthard's Pass. One of the most famous and dramatic of the Alpine passes, St Gotthard's was first traversed by carriage in 1775, although the writings of the English mineralogist Edward Daniel Clarke (1769–1822) suggest that tourists were still a rarity when he took the Gotthard route from Basel to Turin in 1792: 'Our carriages were drawn by oxen and peasants over high mountains of snow, where no European had ever dreamed of meeting a carriage before, among precipices, rocks, torrents and cataracts. The mountaineers beheld us with astonishment, the children ran away from us, and the men could not be kept from the wheels...in their eagerness to see inside.'

To Turner its deserted splendour was the very essence of the Sublime: an unfolding drama of dark clouds and dancing light, determined by the elements and their ever-changing moods. He painted the pass again and again – producing some forty-eight paintings and drawings in all – using techniques that went beyond pictorial accuracy, to convey its essence, its depth, its soul. When I visited, I found an old bridge, the 'Devil's Bridge' of Turner's paintings, a rail bridge and a modern road bridge: the marks of progress. But their collective arrangement, if anything, is even more impressive now the giant waterfall drops hundreds of feet below as trains and lorries are swallowed whole into the mountain. Turner would have painted that.

Ruskin described Turner's *oeuvre* as 'lifting the veil from the face of nature'; revealing its true character both by highly accurate representation – Ruskin claimed to be able to identify the time of day the works were painted by the depiction of the sunlight – and by capturing its emotional intensity, an ability to touch the soul. Ruskin was also in no doubt that Turner's paintings offered lesser mortals a means of experiencing an emotional connection to nature. He brusquely admonished his readers: 'if you…have no feeling for the glorious passages of mingled earth and heaven which Turner calls up before you into breathing tangible being, there is indeed no hope for your apathy, art will never touch you, nor nature inform.'

Ruskin was no alpinist, preferring to draw, record and gaze at the peaks. He was, he boasted, the first tourist to make daguerreotypes of the mountainous scenery. While he was insistent that photography could never be art, he praised its ability to record architectural detail – and, to Ruskin, this was mountain architecture.

But he saw something else in the mountains too. He saw the incredible forms of the mountains – all crags, pinnacles and God-formed peaks – as pure, natural structures, akin to Gothic arches and soaring spires. Where the Enlightenment condemned Gothic as the legacy of a barbarous past, Ruskin viewed it as encompassing the same qualities and values as 'God's work' in the mountains: strength, solidity and aspiration, all written in stone. Just as the caves of Antiparos had, apparently, been the source of perpendicular carved stonework, so the jagged peaks, buttresses and towers of the Alps were in essence the inspiration for the form of Gothic.

Ruskin was also a moralist. Convinced that Victorian society was over-materialistic and in spiritual decline, he saw Gothic architecture as a means of reasserting the pious purity of the Middle Ages – and hence as a route to salvation. He urged his compatriots to turn away from classical architecture – to

seek inspiration from nature as opposed to antiquity and, crucially, to favour the work of good old-fashioned craftsmen over machine-made ornament.

The Gothic Revival in England was already well established in Britain but Ruskin, with his proselytising zeal, did more to transform the aesthetic values and tastes of Victorian society than anybody else. His books, *The Seven Lamps of Architecture* (1849) and *The Stones of Venice* (1851–1853), perfectly captured the *zeitgeist* and were an immediate success. And his reverence for nature and celebration of craftsmanship exerted a powerful influence on architect, designer and socialist William Morris (1834–1896). Morris, like Ruskin, perceived a direct link between moral and social health and architecture and design, and dreamt of skilled creative workers deriving satisfaction from their toil. Inspired by Ruskin's work, he and fellow members of the Arts and Crafts movement, which reached its height between 1880 and 1910, turned to nature for inspiration in their quest for a meaningful style for ninteenth-century architecture, furniture and arts.

Such was Ruskin's phenomenal influence that even an architectural genre was named in his honour: Ruskinian Gothic, a strand of Gothic Revival architecture exemplified in the work of the Irish architectural practice Deane & Woodward. Their Venetian-style Trinity College Museum in Dublin (1852–1857) was hailed as the first true Ruskinian building but their masterpiece was the Oxford University Museum of Natural History (1855–1861). With its polychrome brick and stone, its rich embellishment and high-quality craftsmanship, it set the standard for the public building bonanza of the Victorian age.

Ruskinian Gothic at its very best: the great bulk of the Oxford University Natural History Museum (above) and the Venetian style palazzo of the Museum Building of Trinity College, Dublin (below).

The Alpine Grand Tour and the common man

Before and during the eighteenth century, the Alps – and mountains in general – were viewed with trepidation. Rock falls, landslides and groaning glaciers were deemed to be the work of the devil – or rather devils. The belief that the mountains were inhabited by evil was widespread even among the educated classes. As a result very few people went. And the opinions of the Grand Tourists were fed by the superstitions of the locals – people who lived in mountain communities with strong oral traditions where accounts of freak storms, landslides, avalanches, ball lightning and other perfectly natural phenomena had been collected over the centuries into stories of dragons and demons. We would nowadays explain most of the natural catastrophes of mountains as simply the erosive work of water, wind, ice and gravity: it is the slow return of the peak back to a flat plain. To the medieval mountain farmer, the dragons were responsible.

As late as the early eighteenth century the eminent Swiss scientist Johann Jakob Scheuchzer (1672–1733) published research on the Swiss glaciers, which included reports 'by men of good faith' who had seen dragons in Switzerland. While Scheuchzer himself expressed doubts about dragons' existence, his decision to illustrate his research with fanciful images of them only added credence to the claim. His report was debated by the Royal Society.

So to early Grand Tourists the Alps were not a destination in themselves but a route to Italy – an obstacle to be negotiated as quickly and painlessly as possible. They travelled on inhospitable roads, seldom venturing from the comfort of their carriages. At mountain passes those roads came to an abrupt halt and travelling aristocrats were enthroned in a sedan chair and carried across by local guides. Those of a delicate disposition wore blindfolds to protect them from the full horror of the menacing mountain scenery and the precipitous drop below. This was no place to admire the view. Beauty was to be found in the symmetry of formal gardens or the painterly composition of picturesque pastoral scenes. The seventeenth-century diarist John Evelyn spoke for society as a whole in dismissing the mountainous landscape as 'horrid and fearful crags and tracks'.

By contrast, Ruskin's eulogising of the natural world appealed to a new type of tourist. As a new manufacturing and mercantile class became established and grew richer, and travel became easier with the advent of steam-powered boats and trains, the Grand Tour – inevitably – started to become democratized.

Early backpackers

But it's still surprising to learn that William Wordsworth (1770–1850), our most beloved poet, made the 1,000 mile trip almost entirely on foot. In 1790, at the age of 20, he crossed the Alps on foot with his friend, Robert Jones. Rejecting the comforts of aristocratic travel, they saw themselves as Romantic wanderers, walking some thirty miles a day dressed in peasant clothes with their minimal luggage on their backs. The British backpacker was born.

In stark contrast to the blindfolded aristocrats of an earlier age, this new breed of traveller marvelled at nature's fearsome majesty. Wordsworth translated this awe and fear into poetry, to spectacular effect: his description of crossing the Simplon Pass, which appears in Book VI of his autobiographical magnum opus *The Prelude*, is one of the finest things he wrote.

Poets such as Wordsworth, Byron and Shelley gave the British the language to define a new aesthetic taste. Landscapes, both on the Grand Tour and back

Backpacking in the Alps: while the Romantics established the mountains as a destination in themselves, earlier Tourists viewed them as treacherous territory populated by demons and dragons.

William Wordsworth enjoyed the spartan hospitality of establishments such as the Simplon Hospice. Although his poetry encouraged countless visitors to come to the Alps, he complained in later years about the impact of 'arbitrary, pitiless, godless' tourists.

home in Britain, came to be viewed in a whole new light. The Alps and the Lake District alike became a magnet for visitors in search of natural scenery more awe-inspiring, more fearsome, more Sublime, than the picturesque landscapes of the old Grand Tour.

For Wordsworth, who composed his poetry as he walked, walking was a way of life. The English author Thomas De Quincey (1785–1859) calculated 'upon good data' that over his lifetime 'Wordsworth must have traversed a distance of 175 to 180,000 English miles – a mode of exertion, which to him, stood in the stead of wine, spirits, and all other stimulants whatsoever to the animal spirits, to which he has been indebted for a life of unclouded happiness, and we for much of what is most excellent in his writings.' Walking was a way to get close to nature and close to the common man – a deliberate choice to be left behind in the dust of the aristocratic coach. Not just a means of getting from A to B but a radical, politicized activity.

New roads, bridges and hospices made the Alps much easier to negotiate. The carriage road over the Simplon Pass was constructed in 1800–1807 on the orders of Napoleon.

Above A nineteenth-century engraving of Grand Tourists exploring Mont Blanc and the Aiguilles Rouges. The woman – in what appears to be a crinoline – is being helped by an ingenious arrangement of poles.

Right The sedan chair – the traditional early mode of crossing the Alps. This Grand Tourist is crossing Mount Cenis in August 1775.

Ruskin viewed the Alps as
'mountain architecture',
akin to the arches and spires
of the Gothic architecture
he promoted in his books.

The celebrated view looking north from Mount Rigi.

Conquering the peaks

Walking was also related to climbing. Mountain-climbing came to be seen as an end in itself, another challenge in the unremitting colonial drive to conquer every imaginable territory. In the mid-nineteenth century the Alps enjoyed a Golden Age of mountaineering, starting with Alfred Wills' ascent of the Wetterhorn in 1854 and ending with Edward Whymper's ascent of the Matterhorn in 1865. By the late nineteenth century, having exhausted the supply of new peaks to conquer, mountaineers set their sights on the Pyrenees, the Andes and the Himalayas. Much of the twentieth century saw attention turn once again to new challenges in the Alps: Eiger's North Face and the Drus, the great stacks above the Mer de Glace.

Inevitably smaller peaks became seen as conquerable by everyman and his wife. By 1835 an Englishman, Mr Emery, was organizing trips to Switzerland, shepherding tourists on the 10-day journey from London to Basel for a cost of £20. But it was Thomas Cook who exploited economies of scale to create large-scale package tourism – continental travel at a cost the common man could afford.

Cook's travel empire was made possible by the industrial revolution. His clientele represented a new class of traveller, rich from the fruits of manufacturing and eager to spend their newly acquired wealth. The tools of his trade were steamships and trains – flagship achievements of the technological age. By the 1860s Cook was taking tourists around Switzerland, bringing his charges to the mountains with the help of Europe's new advanced railway system. The prohibitive cost of cutting through the mountains meant that Switzerland was slow to embrace rail travel in the Alps, and the first Thomas Cook travellers had to make the final leg of their journey by carriage.

But the construction of Europe's first mountain railway, from Vitznau to Rigi, in 1871, followed by the Arth to Rigi railway in 1875, transformed Alpine tourism – admittedly at a cost. When the Gotthard Rail Tunnel, the first in the Alps, finally opened in 1882, it had taken 10 years to build, killing 200 workers in the process. A single journey to the summit of Mount Rigi by steam locomotive required 2,200 litres of water and 500 kg of coal – a level of consumption made viable both by the quantity of passengers and the easy availability of fuel.

Cook took his clients from Geneva to Chamonix, to the Bernese Oberland, and finally to Mount Rigi, to climb the summit and admire the prospect from Switzerland's most celebrated vantage point.

Its panoramic vista of mountains and lakes elicited a particularly emotional response from the American writer Mark Twain (1835–1910), who climbed Mount Rigi in 1878. After a three-day trudge during which he lost his way, 'expected to go over a precipice sooner or later', and was irritated by the yodellers pestering him for tips, he finally reached the summit only to find: 'We could not speak. We could hardly breathe. We could only gaze in drunken ecstasy and drink it in.' Exhausted by the 'opiate of Alpine pedestrianism', Twain overslept in his hotel and missed the legendary Mount Rigi sunrise, which was – and remains – the highlight of Thomas Cook's Alpine tours.

The end of the Grand Tour

To the Romantics, the advent of mass tourism was an abomination: insidious proof of industrialisation's malign influence, and an offence against the sanctity of the wilderness. Wordsworth and Ruskin had celebrated the Alps in their writings and yet they both abhorred what was happening as the hordes invaded the countryside. Wordsworth even campaigned to have the railway expansion into the Lake District halted. By 1820, when he returned to the Alps with his wife Dorothy to retrace his earlier tour, was grumbling: 'As to the arbitrary, pitiless, godless wretches, who have removed Nature's landmarks by cutting roads through Alps and Appenines, until all things are reduced to the same dead level, they will be arraigned hereafter with the unjust.' Not that his disappointment dampened his creative ardour: he returned from the trip having written thirty-eight new poems.

By the early 1900s the Grand Tour had lost its exclusivity altogether, undermined by the invention of steam travel and the development of package tourism for a middle-class clientele. In the past the Grand Tour had attracted architects, scientists, writers and poets who wanted to experience the world – to understand and interpret it and use their new-found knowledge to the good of civilisation. Now tourists just wanted a holiday – a stress-free break with a first-class view.

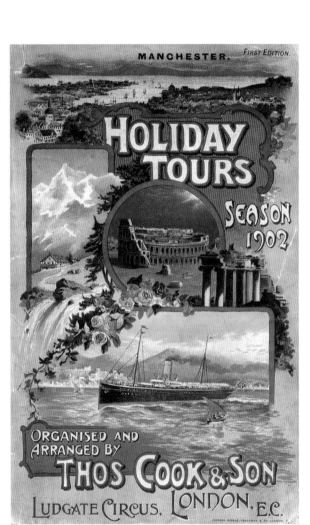

With the emergence of Thomas Cook's empire, the Grand Tour lost its exclusivity and the age of package tourism was born. Souvenirs and images of Mount Rigi and Lucerne were inexpensive and mass-produced.

Luzern vom Gütsch.

Löwe in Luzern.

Rigi-Kulm.

Rigi-Kaltbad.

C.F.PRELL. LIBRAIRIE. LUCERNE
SOUVENIR DU RHIGI

Kaltbad-Känzeli.

Schnurtobel-Brücke.

Vitznau.

Rigi-First.

Rigi-Scheideck.

Rigi-Klösterli.

Arther-Rigibahn.

Arth-Rigibahn & Mythen.

Rigi-Staffel.

Arth-Rigikulm.

Goodbye Greek

Taking the train from Lake Lucerne, through the Alps and back to London is a slow journey. There's a connection in Geneva and another one in Paris. And then there's the cost. For around £550 you can get to and from many European destinations on the train. Add the odd overnight hotel and it isn't difficult to spend ten times what you would on a CheapyJet return ticket.

But that isn't the point. The age of steam killed the exclusivity of the Grand Tour and brought the masses to the great sights. But ironically, travelling by rail still carries with it some of the romance and sense of adventure that early Tourists enjoyed. I choose to travel by rail whenever I can because it's the low-carbon option. But it's also the explorer's option. The iron ways that nineteenth century engineers laid are still there. At every halt or junction there is always an choice, that you never have on a plane, to get off and journey on foot, get out and explore.

Behind the Gothic façade was a stripped-down triumph of engineering, W.H. Barlow's train shed, the largest single-span structure to have been built at the time. Recently restored, it is now the terminal for Eurostar – the modern-day tourist's gateway to the Continent.

Designed by George Gilbert Scott (1811–1878) and opened in 1873, the Midland Grand Hotel stands as testament to a moment in time when Gothic architecture re-emerged from the Middle Ages – and seemed to point the way towards the future.

There is always a view of something. Not an aerial one – views from planes become very repetitive and difficult to identify – but a human-perspective view. And there is, however tenuous, a connection with the speed and and modes of travel of the great European tourists of the past. When I travel by train I feel as though I am properly traversing the ground and giving myself the time to look, think and read about the experiences of others who have been before me. That to me is travel.

And if I have to arrive, then there is no better place in the world than the new Eurostar terminus at St Pancras Station: a cathedral of steel attached to a masterpiece of Gothic architecture. I say this because growing up in Bedfordshire, St Pancras was my gateway to London. It was decrepit, infested with prostitutes and blackened with soot and grime but it was still magnificent and I followed the efforts of John Betjeman to have the place saved from demolition. Constructed in 1868 by the engineer William Henry Barlow, the train-shed boasted the largest single-span structure to have been built at the time, and was a miracle of Victorian engineering. It was matched in magnificence by the eclectic, Gothic Midland Grand Hotel.

Designed by George Gilbert Scott (1811–1878) and opened in 1873, the hotel stands as testament to a period in time when Gothic building, resuscitated from the Middle Ages, represented the most clear-thinking idea of what a British architectural style should be. It seemed to point the way towards the future. Scott confidently predicted that his hybrid architecture – Ruskinian Gothic embellished with other historical styles – would herald a new architectural genre.

The confidence and chutzpah of Scott, however, was in a long line of bullish positions adopted by architects over four centuries. In the early seventeenth century Inigo Jones had announced that Palladian classicism was the future, whereupon it died a death for a century. Wren built St Paul's Cathedral as the apotheosis of classical style led by engineering, pointing to a great age of baroque that Vanbrugh and Hawksmoor would develop for at least, oh, thirty years. Lord Burlington espoused Jones' Palladianism only to see it swamped by fashionable interest in the nonsense of rococo and chinoiserie decorative styles, while Robert Adam, one of Britain's most persuasive national stylists, saw his beloved neo classicism peter out before the end of the eighteenth century. John Soane brilliantly attempted to form a national style by taking classicism and stripping it down but even he only designed a handful of buildings. What followed in the early 1800s was an enthusiastic jamboree of regency styles as 'Hindoo' vied with Turkish and Moorish styles of building and design. And Greek.

The Greek revival was really no more or no less successful than any other building fashion. For a decade or two it seemed to embody the very essence of *civitas*, it was the essential style for public buildings. But its real failing, as with every other imported idea, was that it was patently not of these isles. Where was the sense of 'Britishness' in a style of architecture that had been adopted wholesale by the French for 200 years and recently promoted by Napoleon? Britain in the early nineteenth century was forming a new sense of identity around its colonial expansion and its internal growth as the hotbed of the industrial revolution. The roots of the classical world had been unearthed, mulled over and found wanting. It turned out, perhaps most distressingly of all, that there was no truth in classical architecture just some time-honoured principles and easy-to-follow rules.

This flexibility of Classicism, the ability of this language of a few columns, pilasters, cornices, arches and friezes to adapt to almost any building type and produce a pleasing result, was fully grasped by Inigo Jones. He realised the

The Royal Exchange, London built by William Tite in 1844, a legacy of an era when Greek classicism was deemed to be the style for civic buildings. Reinvigorated Greek classicism inspired the resurgence of Greek architecture by many such as the Danish Hansen brothers who had lived and studied in Athens and spread the gospel in huge and influential public buildings in Athens, Copenhagen and Vienna.

immense variety of buildings you could design using it and saw its potential as a kit of parts. Palladio taught him that. He also clearly saw it as the language of the 'Antients', of the classical world with all the resonance that entailed.

Classical architecture passed through the hands of all the great architects I mentioned above. Each modulated it, found other influences and made classicism his own. Its longevity was stimulated by the tonic of the Grand Tour, administered to each new generation of enthusiasts. But that same longevity led to a bewildering range of interpretations. It's difficult for you and I to spot exactly when a Greek or Roman-inspired building might have been put up. 1630? 1875? In the twentieth century even. That's because those columns and cornices are chewed up and spat out again in yet another arrangement.

Unless you're an historical anorak, it doesn't matter. What is important to recognize, is that despite the relatively short and fashionable life of each of the classical styles (neo classicism, Palladianism, Greek Revival, baroque, Italianate, mannerism, the list goes on), classicism has been amazingly successful at dominating the built environment. It's a survivor. But in the early and mid-nineteenth century its foreignness was its undoing. Britain required a national style. It found inspiration in another architectural order, one that had lain forgotten since the sixteenth century. Gothic.

To be fair, each century has enjoyed one or two mini Gothic revivals in this country. There are Gothic buildings from the sixteenth and seventeenth centuries and one of the most exciting and influential buildings of the eighteenth century turned out to be James Gibbs' Gothic Pavilion at Stowe (now owned by the Landmark Trust and available for you to rent). Influential because placed in its niches are not the statues of saints and bishops, but those of Hereward, Arthur and other British 'Greats'.

Tying an architectural style to Britain's history – no matter how flimsy or bogus – was helpful for the politicians of the nineteenth century. Gothic building would do so many things: help crystallize a national character and pride in our own history counter Enlightenment clarity with the intuition and accessibility of Romantic ideas and deliver a great British icon.

I say it was the politicians because the story of Gothic is neatly told in the commission for London's most famous building, that icon: the Houses of Parliament. The old parliament buildings burned down in 1834, sparking a heated debate as to appropriate style for the new building. Essentially the debate ran: Should it be Greek or Gothic? In the end the neo-classical style, selected in America for the White House and the Capitol, was deemed to reek of

republicanism. In 1835, the Royal Commission charged with responsibility for the rebuilding of the palace, decreed that the appropriate style would be either Elizabethan or Gothic.

A national competition yielded 97 entries, of which all but six were Gothic. The winning entry, by Sir Charles Barry (1795–1860) was a palace in the required medieval style – sort of. It may look Gothic, but Barry had been to Greece on the Grand Tour – and it showed. Instinctively something of a classicist, he relied on sub-contracting Augustus Welby Pugin (1812–52) to design almost every one of the Gothic details and all of the interiors. Aware that his work was essentially a form of window dressing, Pugin would later say: 'All Grecian, Sir... Tudor details on a Classic body.'

Like classicism, the Gothic too, was doomed. The issue of style was already being superseded. The benign capitalist constructors of Bournville, Port Sunlight and Airedale were already redefining architecture in response to function and community needs. A new industrial domestic agenda was being forged. Everyday architecture was evolving into something more practical and responsive. And something else more fundamental was happening. Architecture no longer held sway and was no longer seen as the rightful Ark of the Covenant of civic truth. Ruskin enlarged the scope of his interests to include painting, poetry, craft and manufacturing. William Morris followed. Gothic architecture, preferred for a few decades as the official style of government – although chiefly, in fact, as the official style of a newly-liberated

Greek or Gothic? As the mood shifted, Gothic superceded classicism as the national style. But Charles Barry's design for the Houses of Parliament demonstrates that the distinction was not quite as clear-cut as it appeared. Its Gothic detailing conceals what is essentially a Greek composition. Take away the two towers, and you have a symmetrical building.

British Catholic Church – gave way to the more convincing but less articulate Arts and Crafts movement. The built landscape became inordinately more diverse and even confused.

And perhaps most surprising of all, the concentrated human energy and expression that for over two centuries had found expression in building design, seemed to transfer itself to tunnels, bridges, dams and canals. As Kenneth Clark says in *Civilisation*, the energy and integrity seems to have dropped out of architecture and found itself in a new discipline: engineering. Britain's visual style was rewritten in steel trusses and rivets.

Which is ironic. Because since the early 1600s Grand Tourists had been searching for some kind of hidden truth, some great universal idea that they could bring back and use to somehow improve our own built world. Of course, just by trying, just by copying bits of the layout of sixteenth century Rome, and building banks and town halls that looked like temples, they enriched our towns and cities. But the truth behind Renaissance and then Roman and Greek architecture, if there is one, lies in the basic functionality of stone and wood. The Great Truth is that a triangular roof over our heads needs supports and tree trunks will do. Nails and chocks of wood help. These simple mechanical details became, it seems, enshrined in Greek stone temples.

And so from nails to rivets, beams to trusses, columns to cast-iron posts. The Roman aqueduct became the model for the railway viaduct. The functional language of engineering, something very new and very British, also lay, it turns out, at the roots of classicism. The elusive truth of the Grand Tour is something we can now appreciate every time we take a funicular railway up a mountain, or board a paddle steamer on Lake Lucerne, or board a bus to Naples.

And what can you or I bring back from our own trip? Surely everything's been dug up now, the museums have been long built and there isn't much appetite to build with columns and capitals any more. The adventurism of the Grand Tour has been asphyxiated in the fumes of diesel locomotives and vapour trails and there is nothing more to see.

Wrong. There is everything to see – and be inspired by. The reason Britain has such a fascinating built environment, the reason we have such a rich cultural landscape, is that we have always been a nation of adventurers and risk-takers. Our buildings have historically been interesting, well-made and diverse because we brought back inspiration from foreign places that fired the imagination. Pack your own imagination, and set off to look at any great European building, and you'll discover that within you, the excitement of the Grand Tour still lives.

Further Reading

James Ackerman *The Architecture of Michelangelo*

Robert Adam and James Adam *The Works in Architecture of Robert and James Adam*

Patrick Anderson *Over the Alps: In the Steps of Boswell, Beckford and Byron*

Anon *A New Description of Sir John Soane's Museum*

Tommaso Astarita *Between Salt water and Holy Water*

H. Ballon *The Paris of Henry IV: Architecture and Urbanism*

Andrew Beattie *The Alps: A cultural History*

Guido Beltramini and Howard Burns *Palladio*

J.A. Bennett *The Mathematical Science of Christopher Wren*

Barry Bergdoll *European Architecture 1750–1890*

Frank Brady and Frederick A. Pottle (ed) *Boswell on the Grand Tour: Italy, Corsica, and France, 1765–1766*

Jeremy Black *The Grand Tour*
The Grand Tour in Italy

Thomas Burnet *The Sacred Theory of the Earth*

Lord Byron *Childe Harold's Pilgrimage*

Colen Campbell *Vitruvius Britannicus* (The Classic of Eighteenth-Century British Architecture)

Edward Chaney *The Evolution of the Grand Tour: Anglo-Italian Cultural Relations since the Renaissance*

Edward Chaney and Harold Acton *A Traveller's Companion to Florence*

David Constantine *Early Greek Travellers and the Hellenic Ideal*
Fields of Fire: A Life of Sir William Hamilton

Mavis Coulson *Southwards to Geneva: 200 Years of English Travellers*

Pierre d'Hancarville *The Collection of Antiquities from the cabinet of Sir William Hamilton*

James Davidson *The Greeks and Greek Love: A Radical Reappraisal of Homosexuality In Ancient Greece*

James Dearden *John Ruskin and The Alps*

Brian Dolan *Ladies of the Grand Tour*

Robert Eisner *Travelers to an Antique Land: The History and Literature of Travel to Greece*

John Evelyn and Roy Strong *The Diary of John Evelyn*

Luigi Ficacci *Piranesi*

Brian Fothergill *Sir William Hamilton Envoy Extraordinaire*

Richard A. Goldthwaite *The Building of Renaissance Florence: An Economic and Social History*

Richard Goy *Florence: the city and its architecture*

John Harris and Gordon Higgot *Inigo Jones: Complete Architectural Drawings*

Judith Harris *Pompeii Awakened*

Christopher Hibbert *Florence: The Biography of a City*
The Grand Tour
Rome: The Biography of a City

David Hill *Turner in the Alps: the Journey through France and Switzerland in 1802*

Leo Hollis *The Phoenix*

James Hutton *Theory of the Earth*

Ian Jenkins and Kim Sloan *Vases and Volcanoes: Sir William Hamilton and His Collection*

Ross King *Brunelleschi's Dome: the story of the great cathedral in Florence*

Jordan Lancaster *In the Shadow of Vesuvius*

Michael Leapman *Inigo: The Troubled Life of Inigo Jones, Architect of the English Renaissance*

Ian Littlewood *Sultry Climates*

Elizabeth Longford *Byron's Greece*

Cristina Acidini Luchinat *The Chapel of the Magi: Benozzo Gozzoli's Frescoes in the Palazzo Medici-Riccardi, Florence*

Biran Luckacher *Joseph Gandy: An Architectural Visionary in Georgian England*

Charles Lyell *The Principles of Geology: An Attempt to Explain the Former Changes of the Earth's Surface by Reference to Causes now in Operation*

William L. Macdonald and John A. Pinto *Hadrian's Villa and It's Legacy*

Robert MacFarlane *Mountains of the Mind: A History of a Fascination*

Mary McCarthy *The Stones of Florence & Venice Observed*

Helen Hill Miller *Greece Through the Ages*

Keith Miller *St. Peter's*

François Maximilien Misson *A New Voyage to Italy*

Jemima Morrell *Miss Jemima's Swiss Journal*

Thomas Nugent *The Grand Tour*

Thorsten Opper *Hadrian: Empire and Conflict*

Andrea Palladio *The Four Books of Architecture*

Steven Parissien *Adam Style*

Pausanias *Guide to Greece*

Frederick A. Pottle (ed) *Boswell on the grand tour: Germany and Switzerland, 1764*

Frank D. Prager and Gustina Scalia *Brunelleschi: Studies of his Technology and Inventions*

Bruce Redford *Venice & the Grand Tour*

Jim Ring *How the English made the Alps*

David Roessel *In Byron's Shadow: Modern Greece in the English and American Imagination*

John Ruskin *The Collected Works*
The Nature of Gothic

Witold Rybczyniski *The Perfect House*

Johann Jakob Scheuchzer *Natur-Geschichte Des Schweitzerlandes V2*

Percy. B. Shelley *Hellas, a lyrical drama*

Susan Sontag *Volcano Lover*

Richard Stoneman *Land of Lost Gods: The Search for Classical Greece*

Paul Strathern *The Medici: Godfathers of the Renaissance*

James Stuart and Nicholas Revett *The Antiquities of Athens: Measured and Delineated*

John Summerson *The Classical Language of Architecture*
Inigo Jones

A. A. Tait *The Adam Brothers in Rome: Drawings from the Grand Tour (Paperback)*

Robert Tavernor *Palladio and Palladianism*

Carl Thompson *The Suffering Traveller and the Romantic Imagination*

Adrian Tinniswood *By Permission of Heaven: The Story of the Great Fire of London*

Hugh Tregaskis *Beyond the Grand Tour*

Fani-Maria Tsigakou *The Rediscovery of Greece: Travellers and Painters of the Romantic Era*

Giorgio Vasari *Lives of the Artists*

Vitruvius *Ten Books on Architecture*

Andrew Wilton and Ilaria Bignamini *Grand Tour: The Lure of Italy in the Eighteenth Century*

William Windham *Account of the Glaciers or Ice Alps in Savoy*

William Wordsworth *The Prelude*

Kenneth Woodbridge *The Stourhead Landscape*

Picture Credits

All images by **Hugo MacGregor** except for those listed below.

akg-images: 28 (left) akg-images/Electa; 41 (top right), 65 (bottom) akg-images/Cameraphoto; 76 (bottom) akg-images/Gerard Degeorge; 94, 101 (bottom), 116, 151 (bottom), 175 (top), 196 (bottom), 201 akg-images; 196 (top) akg-images/Erich Lessing; 207 akg-images/historic-maps.

Alamy: 23 © Adrian P. Chinery/Alamy; 26 (top) © Robert Harding Picture Library Ltd/Alamy; 59 (bottom) © Rod Edwards/Alamy; 87 © Carolyn Clarke/Alamy; 163 (bottom left) © John McKenna/Alamy; 200 (right) © Cristina Lichti/Alamy.

Arcaid: 59 top © Richard Turpin/Arcaid; 164 (top) Paul M.R. Maeyaert/Bildarchiv-Monheim/Arcaid; 208-9 Richard Bryant/Arcaid. **Art Archive:** 16 (bottom) The Art Archive/Private Collection/Gianni Dagli Orti; 21 The Art Archive; 26 (bottom), 202 The Art Archive/Bibliothèque des Arts Décoratifs Paris/Gianni Dagli Orti; 58 (left) The Art Archive/Private Collection Italy/Gianni Dagli Orti; 68 The Art Archive/Querini Stampalia Foundation Venice/Alfredo Dagli Orti; 98 (top), 100 The Art Archive/Gianni Dagli Orti; 154-5 The Art Archive/Dagli Orti; 154 (bottom) The Art Archive/National Archaeological Museum Athens/Dagli Orti; 186 (bottom) The Art Archive/University Library Geneva/Dagli Orti.

Bridgeman Art Library: 15 (left) Musée Condé, Chantilly/Bridgeman Art Library; 20 (bottom), 39, 138, 168 (top) Private Collection/Bridgeman Art Library; 22, 104 (right) Yale Center for British Art, Paul Mellon Collection/USA/Bridgeman Art Library; 34 (top) Museo Civico, Turin/Bridgeman Art Library; 45 (left) Bibliothèque de l'Arsenal, Paris/Bridgeman Art Library; 47 (bottom left) Merilyn Thorold/Bridgeman Art Library; 62 (top) Aldo Crespi Collection, Milan/Bridgeman Art Library; 63 (top) Lobkowicz Palace, Prague Castle/Bridgeman Art Library; 77 (bottom) Alinari/Bridgeman Art Library; 95 (bottom right) Alinari/Bridgeman Art Library; 102 (left), 183 (bottom) Private Collection/The Stapleton Collection/Bridgeman Art Library; 123 National Trust Photographic Library/Derrick E. Witty/Bridgeman Art Library; 142 Private Collection/© Agnew's, London, UK/Bridgeman Art Library; 143 (top) Lambeth Palace Library, London, UK/Bridgeman Art Library; 143 (bottom right) Private Collection/Archives Charmet/Bridgeman Art Library, 175 (bottom left), 200 (left) National Portrait Gallery, London/Bridgeman Art Library; 175 (bottom right) Keats-Shelley Memorial House, Rome/Bridgeman Art Library; 187 Kunstmuseum, Basel, Switzerland/Bridgeman Art Library; 194 (top) Maas Gallery, London/Bridgeman Art Library; 197 Abbot Hall Art Gallery, Kendal, Cumbria/Bridgeman Art Library; 199 (top) © Royal Geographical Society, London/Bridgeman Art Library.

British Museum: 168 (bottom), 202 (bottom) © The Trustees of the British Museum. **Corbis:** 19, 46, 148 © Yann Arthus-Bertrand/Corbis; 30 © Sergio Pitamitz/Corbis; 32-33, 169 (bottom) © Atlantide Phototravel/Corbis; 42 (bottom) © Carmen Redondo/Corbis; 47 (top left) © Ivan Vdovin/JAI/Corbis; 48 (top) © Historical Picture Archive/Corbis; 50-51 © Will Pryce/Thames & Hudson/Arcaid/Corbis; 77 (top) © Lee Frost/Robert Harding World Imagery/Corbis; 98 (bottom) © Corbis; 117 © Robert Harding World Imagery/Corbis; 120 © Florian Monheim/Arcaid/Corbis; 169 (top right) © The Gallery Collection/Corbis; 203 (right) © Frank Lukasseck/Corbis.

Michael Dover: 198 (bottom)

Getty Images: 34 (bottom) Imagno/Austrian Archives/Getty Images; 96-97 James L Stanfield/National Geographic/Getty Images; 186 (top) Roger-Viollet/Getty Images; 198 (top) Roger Fenton/Hulton Archive/Getty Images; 209 (right) Hulton Archive/Getty Images.

iStockphoto: 89 (bottom), 212 iStockphoto.

Mary Evans Picture Library: 206 © Thomas Cook Archive/Illustrated London News/Mary Evans Picture Library.

Kevin McCloud: 24, 27 (bottom), 38, 41 (bottom), 43 (bottom), 64 (top right), 89 (top), 101 (top right and left), 103, 124 (bottom), 139 (bottom left), 144 (bottom), 184, 192, 199 (bottom).

Photolibrary: 28 (right) © 2009 photolibrary.com.

Photoshot: 44, 45 (right) © Cuboimages/Photoshot. All rights reserved; 79 World Illustrated/Photoshot All Rights Reserved.

Rex Features: 20 (top) Roger-Viollet/Rex Features; 203 (left) Ruth Tomlinson/Robert Harding/Rex Features.

RIBA: 41 (top left), 48 (bottom), 95 (bottom left), 155 (top and centre left) RIBA Library Drawings Collection; 54 (bottom centre), 81, 95 (top right), 106, 155 (bottom left), 171 (right) RIBA Library Photographs Collection.

Rough Guides: 151 (top right) Michelle Grant/Rough Guides Pictures.

Scala: 40, 52, 54 (bottom right), 55 Photo Scala, Florence; 47 (top right, bottom right) Image copyright The Metropolitan Museum of Art/Art Resource/Scala, Florence; 69 Pediconi/Scala, Florence; 70-71 Photo The Philadelphia Museum of Art/Art Resource/Scala, Florence; 76 (top) Photo Scala, Florence/Fondo Edifici di Culto - Min. dell'Interno; 86 (top) Photo Scala, Florence - courtesy of the Ministero Beni e Att. Culturali; 190 (left) © 2009, White Images/Scala, Florence; 194 (bottom) Digital Image 2009 (c)Hip/Scala, Florence.

Science & Society Photo Library: 113 Science Museum/Science & Society Picture Library.

Sir John Soane's Museum: 108 Sir John Soane's Museum, London

TopFoto: 65 The Granger Collection, New York/Topfoto; 112 Topfoto

First published in Great Britain in 2009
by Weidenfeld & Nicolson
10 9 8 7 6 5 4 3 2 1

A CIP catalogue record for this book is available from the British Library.

ISBN: 978 0 297 85956 7

Design by Andrew Campling and Richard Carr
Picture research by Caroline Hotblack
Editorial by Debbie Woska and Rosemary Anderson
Colour reproduction by Altaimage Ltd
Printed and bound in Italy by Printer Trento Srl and L.E.G.O. SpA

Weidenfeld & Nicolson
The Orion Publishing Group Ltd
Orion House
5 Upper St Martin's Lane
London WC2H 9EA

An Hachette UK Company

The Orion Publishing Group's policy is to use papers that are natural, renewable and recyclable products and made from wood grown in sustainable forests. The logging and manufacturing processes are expected to conform to the environmental regulations of the country of origin.

Mixed Sources
Product group from well-managed
forests and other controlled sources
FSC
www.fsc.org Cert no. CQ-COC-000012
© 1996 Forest Stewardship Council